WATERFALL FINDER'S GUIDE

Western Washington Series

#1. The NORTHERN COUNTIES and OLYMPIC PENINSULA

Robert L. Mooers

WATERFALL FINDER'S GUIDE

Western Washington Series

#1. The NORTHERN COUNTIES and OLYMPIC PENINSULA

Robert L. Mooers

Trail maps by
David S. Tucker
Geological Research Associate
Western Washington University

Fallsguy
Trail Guides

Printed in the United States of America

Cover and interior photographs by Robert L. Mooers
Maps by David S. Tucker

Cover design by Kate Weisel
Book design and prepress: Kate Weisel. www.weiselcreative.com

ISBN 13: 978-0-615-14790-1
Library of Congress Cataloging in Publication Data Pending

Important notice: Please use common sense. No guidebook can act as a substitute for experience, careful planning, the proper equipment, and appropriate training. There is inherent danger in activities involving getting to and viewing the waterfalls represented in this book, and readers must assume full responsibility for their own actions and safety. Changing or unfavorable conditions on ravine edges, or in weather, road, snow, stream-flow levels, or avalanche conditions cannot be anticipated by the author and/or publisher, and are the responsibility of each outdoor participant. Note also that many waterfall chasms have no safety signs or rim barriers and are exceedingly dangerous. The author and/or publishers will not be responsible for the safety of users of this guide.

FALLSGUY TRAIL GUIDES
715 12th Street
Bellingham, WA 98225

www.fallsguytrailguides.com

This book and the poem, *Water On A Wall,* written while at Otter Falls, is for Adena. She is my loving wife, water-falling partner, critical reader, and all around support system.

Water On A Wall

Softly the falling waters flow
While whisper-washing to and fro.
Timelessly, with rhythmic grace
They feather-fall the rock's smooth face.

No frantic plunge from this great height.
All silvered runs and measured flights
They curl and spread, divide and blend;
Aqueous beauty without an end.

Each traveled plume that ends its fall
Is matched anew high on the wall,
Then down it slides to join the deep
In serene Lake Lipsy's cooling keep.

Adena on the superhighway of bushwhacking – a fallen tree.

Acknowledgements

Along the way a lot of people helped this project in both large and small ways. Gas station attendants gave directions, National Forest and National Park employees gladly dragged out maps and literature, and many individuals, of course, were personally familiar with the places I needed to see. More than one fellow-hiker donated a favorite waterfall to the cause. To all of these kind folks, I give my sincere thanks.

Another great 'thank you' goes to David Tucker, friend of long standing, fellow mountaineer, and now a geologist in the role of research associate at Western Washington University. He took a great deal of time away from his volcanology studies of Mount Baker to craft the map graphics for each of the waterfalls in the book.

And right up front in the adulations is my wife Adena. While the business of writing both attracts and repels me, her loving encouragement greatly eased the way.

Contents

Allurement and Danger

The pulse of moving water has always commanded attention, but when its power and grace appear in the more vertical expression of a waterfall, that attraction is transformed into pure enchantment. At low flow a given fall might be a collection of whispering rivulets that divide and blend, splash and spray, even appearing to float rather than plunge when airborne. With spring melt or heavy rains, the same descent may become an enraged and throaty torrent, hurling itself away from the confining rock as if in a bid for its freedom. Thus, a favorite site, visited over and over again, becomes an old friend of many moods.

The fascination of falling water may be found in our appreciation for its natural artistry. It could also spring more simply from an awesome display of raw power. Its real grip on our emotions, though, may lie in a more deeply recessed primal thread, that of the aqueous origin of life on this Earth.

When the warm winds and heavy rains of a "Pineapple Express" bite into the Cascade Mountain snow pack in Western Washington, it's a safe bet that waterfalls are everywhere. Many of these, however, suffer fleeting existences. It is the ones that run for at least three seasons of the year that this book attempts to address.

Omissions from the list are for a variety of other reasons. I decided early on to include only waterfalls that could be visited in a single day. Another parameter is that trail-less routes (bushwhacks) have generally been kept to a quarter of a mile or less. Some waterfalls were left out because their only feasible viewing places were out on ever-steepening brush or moss covered walls where a slip would be deadly.

Some falls were not included only because they did not pop up in the hunt. The locating of waterfalls for inclusion has been enjoyable, but the process could not be all-inclusive; there is no Falling Waters Gazetteer to light the way. Topographic maps were searched at great length. A dozen or more hiking guidebooks, not your usual source of deep reading pleasure, were perused cover-to-cover for their hidden waterfall content. Of course, use was made of the sparse amount of waterfall literature available in libraries and bookstores.

It cannot be over-emphasized that any waterfall presents at least two dangers, those of falling and of drowning. That closer look from the top, or else a plunge into a raging river above or below a waterfall, could be deadly.

Please exercise caution and good judgment. The better views are most often had from the base of the falls anyway, so why climb around the slippery rocks at the top?

Friday Falls, Suiattle River

Navigating This Book

The *Waterfall Finder's Guide, Western Washington Series,* #1, strives to point out all scenically viable waterfalls east to west from the crest of the Cascade Mountains to the Pacific Ocean, and north to south from the Canadian border to and including King County. The presentation begins in Whatcom County. It includes the San Juan Islands and then runs south through Skagit, Snohomish, and King counties to the Seattle area, where it jumps to Aberdeen in order to trace the horseshoe-shaped Olympic Peninsula clockwise along US 101 around to Shelton.

How the Falls Are Grouped

Waterfalls are arranged by major river valley, usually including all of that system's tributaries. In some cases, though, tributaries of the principle stream are prominent enough to be given separate status. The Sauk River off the Skagit, and the Suiattle River, tributary to the Sauk, are cases in point.

All viable falls within each major drainage system are listed as a group under the title of the main river. Supplemental local-name or geographic headings have been added for easier recognition of broad areas.

The falls are presented in an order based on the most logical driving route for getting to them. Thus, a waterfall in the parent stream may be followed by two more along one of its tributaries, *prior* to presentation of the next waterfall in the main stream.

Some waterfall-bearing creeks in western Washington run directly into the Pacific Ocean or into Puget Sound, and are therefore not part of any major river valley. These are grouped by geographic area, such as **San Juan Islands**, or under the name of the nearest city or town. An example of this latter category is Whatcom Creek (in Bellingham) for it sports five nice falls in its four mile run from Lake Whatcom to Bellingham Bay.

Driving Directions

To avoid a great deal of repetition, especially of the more voluminous lists of instructions, **area** driving directions to the primary valley highway associated with each major river valley have been given in the introductions to such headings. These basic directions are then referred to in the

Getting There section of subsequent waterfalls. *Specific* driving directions for the relevant entries will often begin with mileages (or highway mileposts) along that valley highway. When multiple cascades are located along the same road or trail reference may be made to an earlier entry for directions, both driving and walking. A balance has been sought between page-flipping and endless repetitions of directions.

Mileages

Odometers give notoriously different readings. Still, there is often great need for directions in tenths of a mile. Be aware that the mileages given may be a little long or short.

Mileages given as part of continuing directions, driving or walking, will be stated in numerals and will also be cumulative. You might see, "Go left (north) at the 2.3 mile point, and continue to the trailhead on the right side of the road (east) when 6.8 total miles from US 2". Approximate distances that are not part of a cumulative total, ones such as 'a hundred yards', will be stated in words.

Mileposts are those routinely green signs seen along more and more highways. (National park and national forest mileposts are usually brown.) They can be very handy aids, and you will find many references to them in this book. (Abbreviation: **MP**.) They tend to be less useful, however, in the case of national park and national forest roads, when the signs begin their counting at legal boundaries. Milepost 26, for example, only confuses directions when the place is located 14 miles from a major highway.

Milepost numbers will most often have a decimal portion, such as "MP 56.4", meaning that the place is 0.4 mile beyond MP 56. Coming from the opposite direction, the interpretation is 0.6 mile beyond MP 57.

If the access road does not have actual mileposts, or if they are spotty or otherwise unreliable, mileage will be based on readings from an odometer or else taken from a map.

Abbreviations

These have been kept to a minimum. **FR** for forest road, and **SR** for state route, appear frequently in the text. Interstate is nearly always shortened to a capital letter, as in **I**-84 or **I**-5.

Waterfall Names

Names from published sources, especially those from the United States Geological Survey's Geographic Names System, have been respected. So, too, with the names of waterfalls found on local maps and in hiking guidebooks. Some falls on these pages have been labeled by inquiring after local custom. Many, perhaps a quarter of those found in the book, are named after their host waterway. If that, too, is unnamed, the waterfall has been tabbed with a title of the author's own choosing.

The over-riding waterfall names philosophy of this guide is to enjoy the event itself without too strong an emphasis on what it is called.

Information Block

Eight information categories follow each waterfall's name:

Droplet Rating

The droplet rating is a very subjective catchall arrived at by tallying the pluses and minuses associated with a waterfall's natural artistry, its quality of view, and its volume of falling water. Other factors are the intensity (or subtlety) of the drop's sound and the physical difficulties of getting to its site. These judgments will necessarily fluctuate by a couple of droplets with seasonal changes in precipitation and snowmelt. Aesthetics also vary a great deal depending on lighting conditions, seasonal changes in foliage, and relative amounts of woody and earthen debris cluttering the stream.

Waterfalls have been assigned from one to five water droplets with five being practically the ultimate.

These are the intended meanings behind each of the droplet clusters:

 Worth the effort, at least for one visit.

Receives lingering looks, return visits, and perhaps a photograph.

Memorable. Stirs the emotions; may cause you to forget to take pictures.

Unforgettable. Brings on stunned looks or silly smiles, and poetic urges.

Awesome, the perfect ten of hydrokinetics. Apt to cause the viewer to bypass poetry and compose a symphony instead.

Types of Waterfalls

Plunge falls have little contact with rock and drop directly into pools at their bases. **Chutes** are falls more diagonal in character. Because they are confined within rock walls they accelerate over distance rather than drop through space. **Slide** falls are less constricted than chutes and often appear to be more released than propelled; they maintain full contact with the bedrock. **Veils** leave spreading, lacy trails on steeply sloping rock. **Tumbles** take many short, stair-step plunges that hit rocky outcrops and ledges, giving the drop a thrashing, chaotic appearance. A **Flume** is a sliding drop, one deeply etched into cracks or actual geologic faults; these often show much artistry of flow and line and are great places for contemplation.

Two other designations found in the information block address spatial divisions. **Segmented** refers to a cleaving ledge or other obstruction that causes separate flows over the same cliff, and **tiered** means that the height given for the fall occurs in two or more sections separated by short, relatively horizontal stretches. Such divisions can add whole new elements of character and beauty to waterfalls.

Many combinations of the above fall types will be found in the headings. **Plunge/Tumble** falls, for example, are common.

Height of Falls

The height given for a waterfall is its *total* vertical drop, whether it is a single plunge or a series occurring over a run of hundreds of linear feet. Given the very wild characters of some creeks and rivers, it is often difficult to say where one waterfall ends and the next one begins. No rules distinguish rapids from waterfalls, and none suggest that if a horizontal flow between drops is greater than X feet, we must consider the vertical portions to be two separate falls. Thus, many water events in this book have been given height ranges such as from "35 to 65 feet".

Approach

If a vehicle can be taken directly to a waterfall, or within sight of it, the approach will be called a **Drive**. If the on-foot portion is of tourist-attraction standards, that is, with improved surface sidewalks, and when the route is a round-trip distance of not more than a quarter of a mile, it will be termed a **Walk**. If the walking phase is longer than a quarter mile, the approach will be labeled a **Hike**.

A qualifier for certain foot approaches will be that of **No Trail**. For these, popularly called **bushwhacks,** the route will be described in the text. Trail-less routes in the book longer than 0.25 mile are few in number, especially when brush and terrain conditions make them challenging.

Distances are expressed numerically in miles and tenths of miles and are round-trip except when otherwise noted.

Elevations

A **starting elevation** is given for all waterfalls that require more than driving to a parking area. A second number, the **falls elevation**, helps to estimate the overall energy level required in getting to the falls site. Elevation figures are also useful when considering snow-levels in the period from late fall to late spring.

Bushwhacking

Waterfall elevations are far from precise. Those marked on topographic maps by a blue line at right angles to the stream flow stand the best chance of being accurate. Interpolation (i.e., guesswork) still remains in selecting an elevation number *within* the map's contour interval. Elevations determined by altimeter readings will vary plus or minus about a hundred vertical feet.

In the main, falls elevations are intended to be the point at which the stream goes more or less vertical.

Difficulty Rating

The terms **easy**, **moderate**, and **strenuous** describe the overall energy output necessary to get from a vehicle to a view of the falls. **Easy** means the terrain is flat to sloping gently upward and has few obstacles to negotiate. **Moderate** terrain requires effort and a respiration rate above that for such tasks as grocery shopping and strolling. **Strenuous** terrain is steep enough to require frequent pauses and, at times, supplementing hand and toeholds with trees, brush, or boulders.

Long, though otherwise Easy, trails tend to earn Moderate status, and so on throughout the scale.

Seasons For Viewing

This category is of course part guess; it was not possible to visit each of the waterfalls represented in this book in all four seasons. Times of high run-off usually make for more definitive waterfalls. Then too, some waterfalls are at their finest when low water highlights their intricate details. In the listings, the best seasons for viewing are designated as **Sp** for spring, **Su** for summer, **F** for fall, and **W** for winter. Road or trail closures due to snow levels or for wildlife habitat protection may also impact these designations.

Maps

The USGS 7.5′ topographic or other map for each waterfall is listed in order to make your outing safer. At times, in addition to or even in lieu of the USGS sheet, the appropriate Green Trails or Custom Correct hiking map is named.

In addition, an area graphic is included for each waterfall or group of waterfalls. These simple schematics merely clarify the turns, distances, and general layout of an area; they are not to be relied upon for navigation.

Getting There

To avoid needless repetition, driving directions to the principle highway of major river valleys or to geographic areas are given in the introduction to those places. Only specific driving directions appear with each waterfall. They often begin with a mileage figure along the area's principle highway. When multiple cascades are located along the same road or trail you may be referred to driving or walking directions presented with earlier waterfall entries.

Trail and Falls

The **Trail and Falls** section gives walking route information to and from the waterfalls. It describes the character of the terrain encountered, be it steep, rough, brushy, or possibly all of those things. Descriptive notes about each waterfall are added, especially those that pertain to safety of viewing.

Before You Go . . .

As if we needed a reminder, the violent weather of November 2006, sent a strong message. It is possible that some of the roads and trails described here will not be accessible next month, next year, or even now. Please use the **Resources** section, page 213, and check routes before you go.

Lost Lake Outlet Falls, second drop.

Nooksack River Valley

The Nooksack River has three forks, but its wild Middle Fork shows no accessible falls. The primary access for both the North and South Forks and their tributaries is from I-5, exit 255, in Bellingham. The road officially is SR 542, but from Bellingham city limits onward it is more popularly known as Mount Baker Highway.

Hard Scrabble Falls

Type of falls:	Plunge/Tiered
Height of falls:	280 to 310 feet
Approach:	Hike 0.8 mile
Starting elevation:	350 feet
Falls elevation:	620 feet
Difficulty:	Moderate
Seasons for viewing:	Sp, F, W
Map:	USGS Acme 7.5'

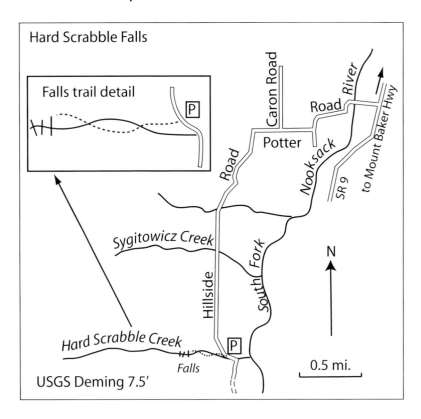

Getting There

Note your mileage when leaving I-5 at exit 255 in Bellingham. Drive east on SR 542 for 14.6 miles and turn right (south) on SR 9. At 16.6 total miles, leave SR 9 for unsigned Potter Road. (West) It is easily located directly on the north side of Everybody's Store. (A destination in itself.) Cross the South Fork Nooksack River Bridge in half a mile and keep going. Pavement ends 19.5 miles from I-5. Three-tenths of a mile farther on, at 19.8 total miles, the gravel road tops out at the second of two rises. Look for a little used woods road on the left (east) and the easily seen trailhead directly across from it on the right (west). There is no trail sign or other marker. Park on the shoulder.

> ***Please note:*** parking as well as trail and falls are located on private property. With good manners we'll always be welcome.

Trail and Falls

A party of settlers named Hard Scrabble Creek and Gulch in August of 1860. They had spent four days climbing only eight miles over Stuart Mountain from Lake Whatcom. When you see the terrain above the falls you will understand both their thinking and their slowness of foot. The trail requires two creek crossings on the way in. At high run-off a person risks wet feet, but real danger is low except to small children. The lower portion of the falls plunges over a broad vertical ledge about 110 feet up. A trail leads steeply upward 0.2 mile from near the base of the lower tier to a second set of drops totaling another 180 feet, but the ascent requires a third and possibly wet crossing of Hard Scrabble Creek. The climb is potentially dangerous. A long rope doubled and draped unknotted from a tree or two will provide a welcome handhold on the descent from the upper tiers.

Racehorse Creek Falls

Type of falls:	Plunge/Tumble
Height of falls:	50 to 80 feet
Approach:	Hike 0.5 mile
Starting elevation:	500 feet
Falls elevation:	560 feet
Difficulty:	Easy
Seasons for viewing:	Sp, F, W
Map:	USGS Kendall 7.5′

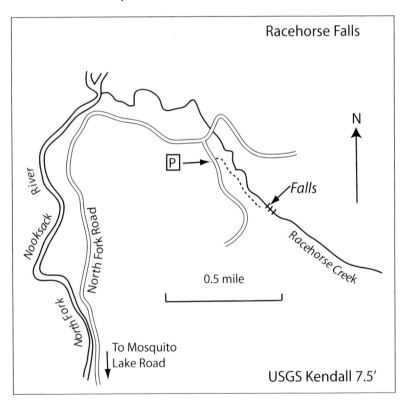

Getting There

From I-5, exit 255 in Bellingham, drive 16.9 miles on SR 542 to the Welcome Store and Mosquito Lake Road, both on the right (south). Reset your odometer and make the turn. In 0.7 mile cross the water-ravaged channels of the North Fork Nooksack River and continue. At 0.9 mile turn left (east) onto the North Fork Road, paved to the 3.3 total mile mark. The gravel road passes through badly mauled clear cut forest for the remainder of the way.

A gate at 3.5 miles is most often open. (If not, the falls trailhead is only a 3.8 mile round-trip walk from parking near the gate.) Drive on; with the wooden bridge over Racehorse Creek in sight, turn right (south) onto a side road at the 5.0 mile point. In a short distance, less than two tenths of a mile, park in a large, often trashy turnout on the right-hand side of the road.

Trail and Falls

The trail, though unsigned, is easily located on the left (east) side of the road opposite the parking area. It is unmaintained and rough, often with many blown-down trees across its path, but is not difficult to locate. In contrast to the flat approach of both road and trail, the waterfall is a surprise. At the base of the plunge portion, the now tumbling stream enters a rock-walled mini-canyon before gushing into a placid summertime swimin' hole.

Maple Falls

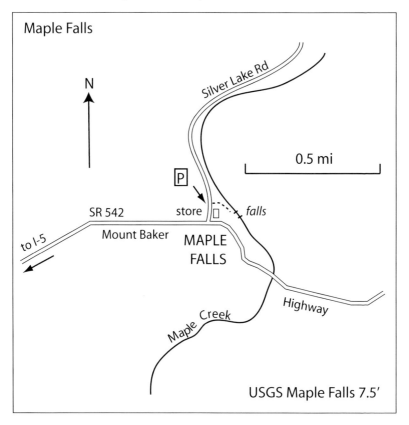

Type of falls:	Chute/Flume
Height of falls:	40 to 50 feet
Approach:	Walk 0.1 mile
Falls elevation:	550 feet
Difficulty:	Easy
Seasons for viewing:	Sp, F, W
Map:	USGS Maple Falls 7.5'

Maple Falls

N

Silver Lake Rd

0.5 mi

P

SR 542   store   falls

to I-5   Mount Baker   **MAPLE FALLS**

Maple Creek   Highway

USGS Maple Falls 7.5'

Foxglove in November

Getting There

From I-5, exit 255, in Bellingham, drive east on SR 542 for 25.8 miles to the community of Maple Falls. Turn left on Silver Lake Road, but only far enough to park at the northern end of the long commercial building on the northeast corner of the intersection.

Trail and Falls

At the rear of the paved parking lot is a chain-link fence that confines a Department of Transportation facility. Locate a path beside the fence through tall grass and follow them both eastwards away from parking. When the fence turns right (south) continue a few steps east and find the short trail down into the trough of Maple Creek.

The waterfall takes three flume-like chuting, sliding, and tumbling drops through a pleasant rocky grotto.

Nooksack Falls

Type of falls:	Plunge
Height of falls:	165 feet
Approach:	Walk 0.1 mile
Falls elevation:	1480 feet
Difficulty:	Moderate
Seasons for viewing:	Sp, Su, F, W
Map:	USGS Bearpaw Mtn. 7.5'

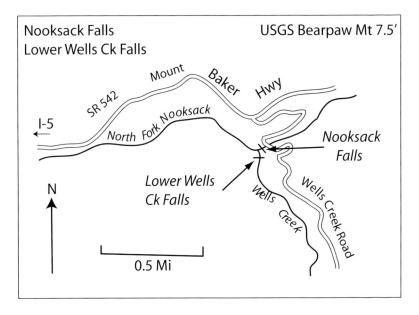

Getting There

Leave I-5 at Bellingham exit 255 and drive east on SR 542. At 40.7 miles turn right onto Wells Creek Road. Nooksack Falls is found 0.5 mile downhill. Ample parking is provided immediately upstream of the falls on both sides of the bridge over the North Fork Nooksack River.

The Falls

At moderate to high flow levels, twin columns of water make the awesome leap. Turbulent Wells Creek drops into the river at the base of the higher falls, and a portion of its waters turn sideways, if not actually upstream, to join the larger fall's plunge pool.

A chain-link fence provides safe viewing, but every two to three years a fatality occurs at this popular attraction as people insist on getting out on the brink. There are boot-driven routes to good view sites which go down along the fence, but these require a bit of athleticism. Thirty yards back from the bridge (north) easier pathways lead to the same good fenced views.

Lower Wells Creek Falls

Type of falls:	Tumble
Height of falls:	30 feet
Approach:	Walk 0.1 mile
Falls elevation:	1350 feet
Difficulty:	Moderate
Seasons for viewing:	Sp, Su, F, W
Map:	USGS Bearpaw Mtn. 7.5'

Getting There

Follow the driving directions for Nooksack Falls.

The Falls

Walking and viewing directions are the same as for Nooksack Falls, the previous entry. Lower Wells Creek Falls enters the Nooksack River at the base of the larger drop.

Winter slide debris, road/trail to Wells Creek Falls

Wells Creek Falls

Type of falls:	Plunge
Height of falls:	90 feet
Approach:	Drive or Hike 9.2 miles (see below)
Starting elevation:	1480 feet
Falls elevation:	2600 feet
Difficulty:	Moderate
Seasons for viewing:	Sp, F
Map:	USGS Mount Baker 7.5'

Getting There

Leave I-5 at Bellingham exit 255. Drive east to MP 40.7 of SR 542, and turn right (south) on Wells Creek Road. In 0.6 mile park at a gate just beyond the bridge at Nooksack Falls.

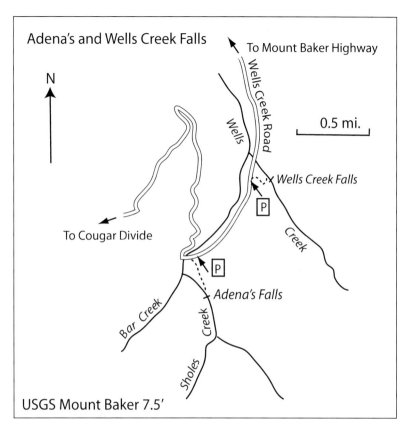

Adena's and Wells Creek Falls

N

To Mount Baker Highway

Wells Creek Road

Wells

0.5 mi.

Wells Creek Falls

P

To Cougar Divide

Creek

P

Adena's Falls

Bar Creek

Creek

Sholes

USGS Mount Baker 7.5'

Trail and Falls

Pretty Wells Creek Falls is visible in the distance from Wells Creek Road with a 9.2-mile round-trip walk or drive from the bridge over the North Fork Nooksack River at Nooksack Falls. For eight months of the year, in the interest of protecting mountain goat habitat, Wells Creek Road is gated about 0.1 mile beyond Nooksack Falls. From July 1 through October 31 the road is open to motor vehicles. Walking, bicycling, and cross-country skiing are permitted any time conditions allow. Mountain goats are frequently seen on the steep, rocky ridge to the east of the gravel road.

Wells Creek Falls could easily be bypassed, so look for this particular set of circumstances: At approximately 4.3 miles from Nooksack Falls, Wells Creek Road begins a downhill glide. Icy Peak, Mount Shuksan, and Mount Baker come into view ahead and to the right (southwest) in the

11

same vicinity. In the foreground of that view is the extremely braided channel of Wells Creek. (Upstream of the entry of Wells Creek the same braided channel has become Bar Creek.) At the bottom of the road's descent, 4.6 miles from the (open or closed) gate just beyond Nooksack Falls, Wells Creek passes deeply beneath the road via a culvert.

Standing over the culvert, look upstream about a quarter mile along Wells Creek for a somewhat screened view of the 90-foot plunge fall.

A good view is possible with a trail-less approach. Continue south along the road about 150 feet from the culvert to a gravel embankment on the left. Boot tracks go up the gravel and are traceable for a short way into the woods. From there on, choose your own best route through the maze of brush and downed trees. The best views are from the top of a steep slope on the downstream side of the plunge pool.

Plan for 6 or 7 hours if walking in. Carry binoculars to look for goats.

Adena's Falls

Type of falls:	Plunge
Height of falls:	140 to 150 feet
Approach:	Hike 0.6 mile, no trail
Starting elevation:	2640 feet
Falls elevation:	2960 feet
Difficulty:	Strenuous
Seasons for viewing:	Su, F
Map:	USGS Mount Baker 7.5'

Getting There
Follow the driving directions for Wells Creek Falls, (previous page). Parking for Adena's Falls is along Wells Creek Road at the east end of the bridge over Bar Creek, and only 0.8 mile beyond the culvert crossing of Wells Creek.

Trail and Falls
Ninety-five percent of this bushwhack is easy, the other five is tough. Some rudimentary trail-work on the way up from the road, along with a slew of steps down into steep Sholes Creek canyon, would quickly turn

Adena's Falls into a five-dropper. It is nonetheless a classic plunge-pool beauty.

Follow these guidelines closely and you should have no problems. Walk to the far end (west) of the curved bridge over Bar Creek and stand at the beginning of the structure on its downstream side. Look kitty-corner to the opposite or upstream end of the east side of the bridge. Looking upward from that line, actually a bit left of the line, the low-point on the skyline marks the trough of Sholes Creek.

Although magnetic compass navigation is not called for here, such a directional aid-finder would be a big help. The "line" you need is a true bearing of 150 degrees. If you do use a compass, stand well back from the steel components of the bridge while taking the sighting. Ferrous metals of any origin can raise havoc with results.

Seventy-five feet east of the bridge, turn right (southward) and climb the steep bank of the road-cut to where a hole in the dense brush forced by others makes a good start toward the waterfall. (Some orange flagging ribbon may still be seen there.) Cut to the right soon to get into the nearly brush-free maturing timber. (Speaking of flagging ribbon, it is a good idea to bring some along to mark your own way on any trail-less adventure. It is a huge help because things certainly do look different on the way out.)

The demarcation between the thick brush of the more recent clear cutting on the left (northeast) and the nearly vegetation-free forest floor of the older trees is maintained nearly as far up as one must climb. At 2,800 to 2,860 feet in elevation, move right (southwest) without rising higher until on the steep lip of Sholes Creek canyon. **Note:** If you start too low, i.e., get into the canyon too soon, too much side-hilling will have to be done, some of it dangerous. If too high, the side-hilling becomes the vertical rock of the waterfall's vast plunge-pool wall. There is a happy medium where some steep down-gouging along the base of the cliff will get you to the plunge pool. Descending anywhere else approaches foolhardiness.

Sholes Creek drops forty feet from the brink to a tilted saucer, and then leaps another hundred feet to a frothy landing in the creek bed below. A short way downstream it does it again, launching itself another sixty- to one- hundred or more feet downward. This second event seemed a bit remote from the main attraction to be included in its total drop. Also mighty dangerous, and Adena's Falls doesn't need any puffing up.

Bagley Creek Falls

Bagley Creek Falls

Type of falls:	Plunge/Chute
Height of falls:	35 to 45 feet
Approach:	Hike 0.3 mile
Starting elevation:	2440 feet
Falls elevation:	2450
Difficulty:	Easy
Seasons for viewing:	Sp, Su, F
Map:	USGS Mount Larrabee 7.5′

Getting There

Leave I-5 at Bellingham exit 255. Head east on SR 542. Soon after crossing the North Fork Nooksack River for the second time, turn left (east) into a large snow-park lot 46.8 miles from I-5. The turn is directly opposite the entrance to Silver Fir Campground. Reset your mileage at the start of FR 3070 (also known as Razor Hone Road). The forest road will be found in the left rear of the two- to three-acre parking area.

There are lots of side roads, but FR 3070 is easy to follow for it is the only one with a crushed rock surface. Encounter a Y at 1.7 miles. Go right (southeast) and uphill on FR 020, also of crushed rock. Though narrow and brushy, its surface is good. The crushed rock, along with the drive-ability, gives out at 2.4 miles. The turn-around is small, but there is space for three or four vehicles without blocking the roadway.

Trail and Falls

See the Trail Map on next page. Since it is only a stretched tenth of a mile from a prepared ski-way, this pretty little interlude is also reachable on cross-country skis. (During one visit, it was complete with a yearling, falls-viewing black bear.)

Walk the still discernible old roadway a bit more than 0.1 mile. Where it curves left (eastward) and begins to fade, the falls will be heard on the right. There is an approximately fifty-foot section of mostly brushless as well as trail-less going from the diminishing roadway to the bank of Bagley Creek. The waterfall and its rock-walled grotto are just upstream. The best views of both are close to where they are first seen.

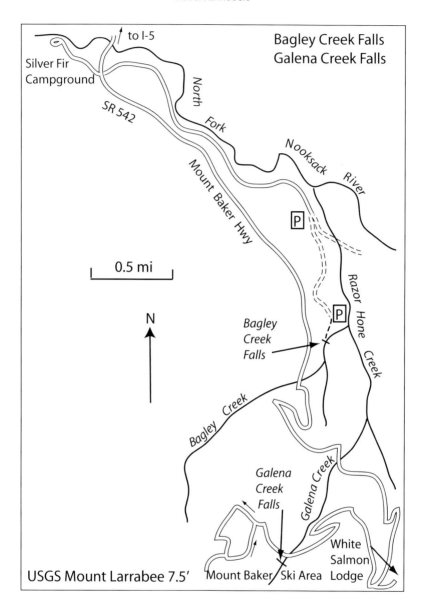

Bagley Creek Falls
Galena Creek Falls

Silver Fir
Campground

to I-5

SR 542

North Fork

Nooksack River

Mount Baker Hwy

P

Razor Hone Creek

0.5 mi

N

Bagley
Creek
Falls

P

Bagley Creek

Galena
Creek
Falls

Galena Creek

White
Salmon
Lodge

USGS Mount Larrabee 7.5'

Mount Baker Ski Area

Galena Creek Falls

Type of falls:	Tumble
Height of falls:	25 feet
Approach:	Drive
Falls elevation:	3840 feet
Difficulty:	Easy
Seasons for viewing:	Sp, Su, F
Map:	USGS Mount Shuksan 7.5′

Getting There

Leave I-5 at Bellingham exit 255. Drive east on Mount Baker Highway (SR 542) for 53.6 miles. Park near the bridge spanning Galena Creek. It will be found 0.3 mile before the road arrives at Highwood and Picture Lakes at Heather Meadows. The waterfall is within the bounds of Mount Baker Ski Area.

The Falls

The waterfall, located a short distance upstream from the concrete bridge over Galena Creek, tumbles over the exposed ends of vertical, six-sided basalt columns. (This hexagon crystalline formation is the result of slow cooling of lava flows, and is common near volcanoes.)

Galena Creek is fed by snowmelt, and the waterfall is therefore at its best in late spring. At times in winter the scene is magnificent, but is more often completely frozen over or buried beneath heavy snows.

The gorgeous mountain visible from the winding drive up to Galena Creek is *not* Mount Baker. It is equally impressive Mount Shuksan. (Don't feel lonely if you assumed otherwise; the author has a commercially produced post card which tags it as Mount Baker.)

Bellingham - Chuckanut Mountain Area

In May of 1999 the rupture of a gasoline pipeline crossing Whatcom Creek spilled some 200,000 gallons of the volatile fluid into the water. An explosion and fire followed. Transported rapidly by the fast flowing waters, the conflagration raced 1.5 miles downstream, snuffing out three human lives and burning one creekside home to the ground. Most trees within a hundred feet of the creek were blackened, and virtually all organisms in the stream perished. The aftermath is most evident at the second entry in this series of waterfalls, but creekside vegetation is making great strides in recovering.

Whatcom Creek runs from Lake Whatcom to Puget Sound in only 4 miles, but in its first 1.4 miles it manages to lose about two hundred-fifty of the three hundred-fifteen vertical foot difference between the fresh and saltwater bodies. There are five worthy waterfalls along the way, though only three have official names.

To reach Whatcom Creek, leave I-5 at Bellingham, exit 253, signed Lakeway Drive.

Roeder Falls

Type of falls:	Tumble
Height of falls:	25 Feet
Approach:	Walk 0.2 mile, wheelchair accessible
Starting elevation:	10 feet
Falls elevation:	45 feet
Difficulty:	Easy
Seasons for viewing:	Sp, F, W
Map:	USGS Bellingham North 7.5'

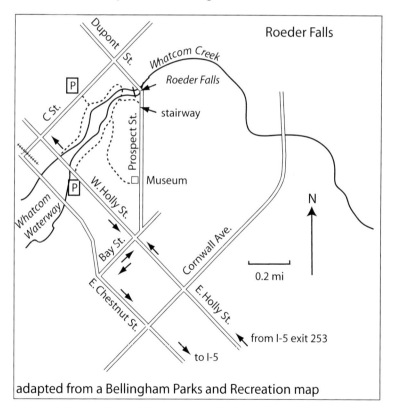

adapted from a Bellingham Parks and Recreation map

Getting There

In Bellingham, take I-5 Lakeway exit 253. From the south, go right at the bottom of the ramp for one long block on King Street to Lakeway Drive and turn right (west). Arriving from the north, the exit ramp goes directly to Lakeway Drive. Turn right (west). Reset your odometer. After crossing Ellis Street the way becomes East Holly Street and continues down a long hill through town. At 1.1 miles, a bit more if you came up the interstate from the south, find on-street parking in the vicinity of the bridge over the mouth of Whatcom Creek. Maritime Heritage Park occupies portions of both sides of the waterway. For alternative on-street parking proceed along the now *West* Holly and turn right (east) on C Street. About a block and a half up hill park near the obvious northern entrance to the waterfall trail.

Trail and Falls

Walking directions are from the more southerly side of the creek. With Whatcom Creek in sight, follow the paved walkway northeasterly and upstream. Along the route there is a delightfully signed collection of indigenous trees, shrubs, and plants. The top of the falls, more accurately a long rapid, is less than 0.2 mile from West Holly Street, but a bridge over the tumult at the 0.1 mile point provides a nice view. It also offers a loop return to parking. Henry Roeder, the city's first white settler, built a sawmill on this site in 1852.

Middle Whatcom Falls

Middle Whatcom Falls

Type of falls:	Plunge
Height of falls:	15 feet
Approach:	Hike 0.8 mile
Starting elevation:	100 feet
Falls elevation:	120 feet
Difficulty:	Moderate
Seasons for viewing:	Sp, F, W
Map:	USGS Bellingham North 7.5′

Getting There

Leave I-5 at exit 253, Lakeway Drive, the same as for Roeder Falls except turn left (east) at Lakeway Drive. At a traffic light in a bit over 1.0 mile, turn left (north) on Yew Street. Yew quickly becomes Woburn Street, but the change is otherwise unnoticed. At just under two miles Woburn crosses Whatcom Creek, and the falls trailhead is found a bit beyond at the intersection of Woburn, Iowa, and another piece of Yew Street. Nearby on-street parking is tight to non-existent. No official trailhead parking is found either, but a pair of small (though unsanctioned) opportunities exist. At approximately 1.7 total miles from I-5, and a little before crossing Whatcom Creek, there are two service roads in succession on the right side (east) of Woburn Street. One is gated and the other is blocked with boulders, but there is space for two to three vehicles in each place without blocking a right of way. *No parking* signs were not in evidence at the time of our visit, but good driving and parking manners always rule.

Trail and Falls

See the Trail Map on next page. Walk north on the Woburn Street sidewalk for a quarter mile to the four-way intersection. While crossing the bridge over Whatcom Creek, take time to look both up and downstream at the swath of burned-out trees. The carnage is less obvious as healing takes place, but for years to come it will remain as evidence of mankind's mocking of fair play in a sustainable relationship with Earth. Downstream, a new, browntone home stands on the south bank, where the previous one was consumed by the racing fireball.

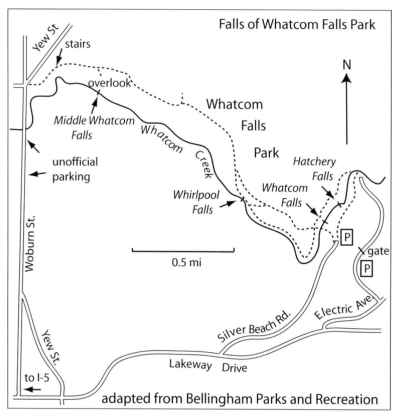

At the four-way street intersection, walk right (east) on a graveled path leading to a long flight of stairs. Just beyond the top are two viewing platforms for observing the devastated creek valley. In another 0.1 mile eastward a side path goes to the right (south) to tree-strained views of the modest waterfall. The drop is only about fifteen feet, but in full flow is an impressive plunge across a seventy-foot width of ledge.

The main falling-water event in the park, Whatcom Falls, follows as a separate entry, but that larger waterfall is also a delightful round-trip walk of slightly more than two miles from the viewpoint for Middle Whatcom Falls. And on the way you may also detour slightly to see the Whirlpool. For the through-the-park route continue eastward on the same wide, graveled pathway. At 0.7 total miles from parking, a trail spur on the left (north) is a park entrance at the end of St. Clair Street, and at 0.9 miles there is another at Erie Street. Bear right at each to stay on course.

A sort of Y occurs at 1.0 mile. Continue straight ahead for the direct route to Whatcom Falls. Or take the unsigned right fork, a short stairway downward, and be looking into The Whirlpool a tenth of a mile later. From there, follow the creek up stream on equally good pathway to the old stone bridge across the creek at Whatcom Falls, 1.3 miles from the trailhead.

Whatcom Falls

Type of falls:	Segmented Plunge
Height of falls:	25 feet
Approach:	Walk 0.1, wheel chair accessible
Starting elevation:	270 feet
Falls elevation:	250 feet
Difficulty:	Easy
Seasons for viewing:	Sp, Su, F, W
Map:	USGS Bellingham North 7.5'

Getting There

Both Whatcom Falls and The Whirlpool can be reached with an extended hike from Middle Whatcom Falls, presented previously.

For driving directly to Whatcom Falls, leave I-5 at Bellingham exit 253, and go left (east) on Lakeway Drive. (Note that the off-ramp for northbound drivers ends into King Street, where a right turn, south, leads to Lakeway Drive in one long block. From there, turn left onto Lakeway at the light.) At about 1.4 total miles, depending on whether you came via I-5 north or I-5 south, turn left at a traffic signal onto Silver Beach Road. The turn is signed for Whatcom Falls Park. Reach the parking area at the 1.8 total mile mark from I-5. (There are rest rooms a short walk up behind the covered picnic pavilions to the right of the parking area.)

Trail and Falls

The falls can be viewed via a short, moderately steep paved walk down to a picturesque stone bridge over Whatcom Creek.

The Whirlpool

Type of falls:	Chute/Plunge
Height of falls:	12 feet
Approach:	Hike 1.0 mile
Starting elevation:	270 feet
Falls elevation:	190 feet
Difficulty:	Easy
Seasons for viewing:	Sp, F, W
Map:	USGS Bellingham North 7.5'

Getting There

Follow the driving and parking directions for Whatcom Falls. See the Trail Map on page 22.

Trail and Falls

The walkway leading down to Whatcom Falls and the stone bridge across Whatcom Creek are plainly evident on the north side of the paved parking area. Cross the bridge and go left at a fork to follow a wide pathway downstream. At just under 0.2 mile, a short loop trail goes to the left onto a rocky point at a bend in the creek, but quickly rejoins the main trail. At 0.4 mile the way intersects a pipeline creek-crossing of the infamous rupture and explosion covered in the introduction to Bellingham Area waterfalls.

There is a fork in the trail just beyond. (The left tine leads to a footbridge over Whatcom Creek and then, in a bit under a mile westward, to Woburn Street within a few hundred feet south of parking for Middle Whatcom Falls.) Go right at the fork (northwest) and look down into The Whirlpool 0.5 miles from parking.

Hatchery Falls

Type of falls:	Plunge/Chute
Height of falls:	20 feet
Approach:	Hike 0.3 mile
Starting elevation:	720 feet
Falls elevation:	750 feet
Difficulty:	Easy
Seasons for viewing:	Sp, F, W
Map:	USGS Bellingham North 7.5'

Getting There

Follow the driving directions for Whatcom Falls. Parking and the trailhead are the same. See the Trail Map on page 22.

Trail and Falls

Take note of the fish hatchery at the eastern end of parking and walk the paved road in that direction as it follows the south bank of Whatcom Creek. Two waterfalls are near the hatchery; both apparently too upstaged by Whatcom Falls to have been graced with names. The first is an 8-foot plunge fall and the second, a bit farther upstream (designated here as Hatchery Falls) is a 20-foot plunge and chute combination. Stream access on the south bank is via impromptu footpaths.

Prospector Falls

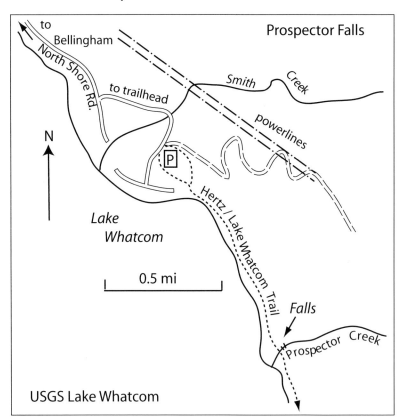

Type of falls:	Plunge/Slide
Height of falls:	45 Feet
Approach:	Hike 2.0 miles
Starting elevation:	370 feet
Falls elevation:	360 feet
Difficulty:	Easy
Seasons for viewing:	Sp, F, W
Map:	USGS Lake Whatcom 7.5′

Prospector Falls

to Bellingham

North Shore Rd.

to trailhead

Smith Creek

powerlines

P

N

Hertz / Lake Whatcom Trail

Lake
Whatcom

0.5 mi

Falls

Prospector Creek

USGS Lake Whatcom

Getting There

From the south, leave I-5 at Bellingham exit 253. Drive east on Lakeway Drive for 1.7 miles to a Y. (1.9 miles if exit 253 was approached from the north.) Go left (northeast) on Electric Avenue to Electric's continuation as North Shore Drive at 2.9 total miles. (Alabama Street enters from the left, or west.) Lake Whatcom will be in view to the right for seven more miles, during which North Shore Drive becomes North Shore Road. At 10.2 miles a permanent detour (left) has been built around a serious Smith Creek road washout. Go left there and drive another half-mile to a large parking area for North Lake Whatcom Trailhead, 10.7 miles from I-5.

Trail and Falls

The trailhead for the Hertz Trail (to the falls) is very close to the historic site of Sunnyside, a settlement-era logging community which was the earlier starting point for an 1860 cross-mountain gold prospecting trip. The title "Prospector Falls" honors not so much the group's purpose as its grit. The rugged terrain forced the party to spend four days clawing its way the six miles over the mountain to the South Fork Nooksack River.

The Hertz Trail, formerly the Lake Whatcom Trail, starts midway along the south margin of the parking area. An alternate trail leaves to the left (south) off a powerline road just inside its gate. (The trail choices rejoin in a little more than a quarter mile. Walking distance either way is about the same.) The lakeside is reached in 0.3 mile, where a nicely designed informational pavilion straddles the trail. The route uses the bed of the logging and coal-hauling railroad that served the mines of Blue Canyon, located at the south end of the twelve-mile long glacial lake. The double-drop waterfall is found at 1.0 mile.

A second waterfall is located nearly 0.5 mile farther south, but its flow is too seasonal for serious consideration. The Hertz Trail goes on for a round trip of eight scenic miles, but the walk ends with the coldness of a chain-link fence signed as private property.

Austin Creek Falls

Type of falls:	Slide/Tumble
Height of falls:	20 feet
Approach:	Drive
Falls elevation:	470 feet
Seasons for viewing:	Sp, W
Map:	Bellingham City Map, Whatcom County Map (showing Sudden Valley)

Getting There

From the south, take I-5 Alger exit 240 and drive east 0.8 mile to cross Old Pacific Highway at the Alger Bar and Grill. In 6.8 total miles stay left at a Y. When 8.7 miles from I-5, with Sudden Valley in sight, turn left (west) on Lake Louise Road. Drive an additional half mile to Gate 5, one of Sudden Valley's numerous entrances. Turn left (west) through the gate. Shortly uphill take a right (north) onto Tumbling Water Drive, and in less than a tenth of a mile (9.4 miles from I-5) park on the left before the bridge over Austin Creek.

From the north, take I-5 Lakeway Drive exit 253 and go (east). Stay right at a fork when Electric Avenue goes left. Lakeway Drive changes names several times, but opt for the main flow of traffic and you won't even notice. (Ignore Old Lakeway Drive.) At 3.5 miles from 1-5 and half way down steep Cable Street (with Lake Whatcom in view) turn right (south) on Austin Street. Continue straight up hill after a four-way stop where the way becomes Lake Louise Road. At 7.5 miles from I-5 turn right into Sudden Valley Gate 5. Go up a gentle hill for a tenth of a mile, turn right on Tumbling Water Drive, and coast to a parking area on the left before crossing the bridge over Austin Creek.

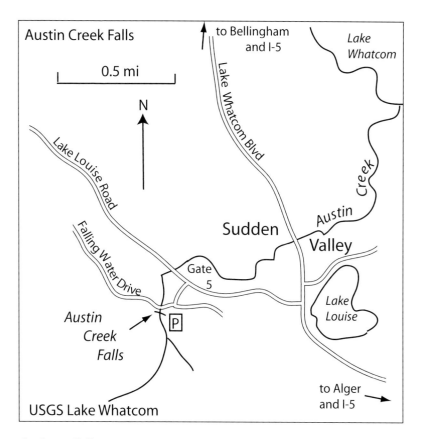

Trail and Falls

Austin Creek Falls is a place of restful beauty. Three sliding, tumbling drops show a pleasing line with a whispered voice that speaks of tranquility. For a bonus – if the crumbling way is negotiable – a crude trail leads up and out of the parking area and down again to gentle rapids above the falls. It's only 0.2 mile in and out and it has someone's *secret place* written all over it. Don't walk it, however, unless you enjoy trails that are slippery, steep, and rough.

The falls and all roads inside Sudden Valley's gates belong to the Sudden Valley Association. The public is welcome, but please bring good manners with you so the welcome mat is not withdrawn.

Padden Creek, First Falls

Type of falls:	Flume/Slide
Height of falls:	20 to 25 feet
Approach:	Hike 1.0 mile
Starting elevation:	450 feet
Falls elevation:	400 feet
Difficulty:	Easy
Seasons for viewing:	Sp, W
Map:	USGS Bellingham South 7.5'

Getting There

Lake Padden Park and the lake's outlet stream, Padden Creek, are reached by way of I-5 in Bellingham. From northbound I-5, take exit 252 and turn right (south) 1.9 miles on Samish Way to the park's west entrance. [Southbound exit 252 also puts you on Samish Way. Turn left (east) to cross over the freeway and then right (south) to the park.] (The distance to Lake Padden Park west entrance from the southbound off-ramp is 2.2 miles.) Once through the gate, continue past the rest rooms to park just beyond the tennis courts.

Trail and Falls

Walk west on the paved park road a short distance, then leave the road, left, to join a wide graveled portion of the around-the-lake walking path. In just 0.2 mile it crosses Padden Creek at the lake's outlet, but do not cross the bridge; turn right instead on a wide trail along the northeast bank of the creek. First Falls, a gentle slide over bedrock, is reached in a bit over 0.5 mile from parking.

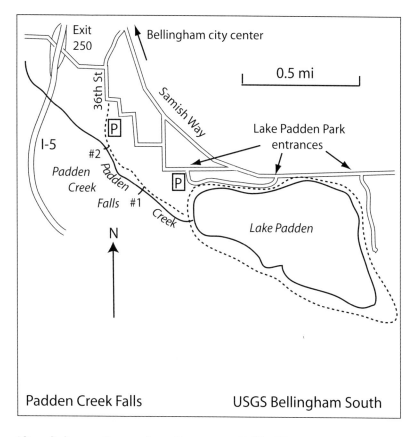

Padden Creek Falls   USGS Bellingham South

Padden Creek, Second Falls

Type of falls:	Tumble
Height of falls:	50 to 60 Feet
Approach:	Hike 1.5 miles*
	* (0.6-mile round trip from Padden Creek, First Falls)
Starting elevation:	450 feet
Falls elevation:	360 feet
Difficulty:	Easy
Seasons for viewing:	Sp, W
Map:	USGS Bellingham South 7.5'

Getting There
Follow the driving directions for Padden Creek, First Falls. See Trail Map on previous page.

Trail and Falls
Continue downstream from Padden Creek, First Falls. Stay left at a trail split in less than 0.2 mile, then look for the diminishing remains of a small, collapsed wooden structure on the left. The waterfall is just downstream from the ruins. Views from the trail are sketchy, but a more appreciative one requires a steep, loose-soils descent to the creek bed. The way is not particularly dangerous, only nasty.

When back to the lake, why not turn right to cross Padden Creek and circumnavigate the lake? It's a total of only 2.4 additional miles and will mysteriously bring you right back to the parking area. How did they *do* that?

Lost Lake Outlet Falls

Type of falls:	Slide/Plunge
Height of falls:	80 Feet
Approach:	Hike 7.8 miles
Starting elevation:	1400 feet
Falls elevation:	1180 feet
Difficulty:	Moderate
Seasons for viewing:	Sp, F, W
Map:	USGS Bellingham South 7.5'

Getting There
From the south, take I-5 Exit 231 in Burlington and drive north on SR 11, Chuckanut Drive. A few feet north of MP 16 turn right (east) onto Hiline Road.

From the north, take I-5 Exit 250, the northern end of SR 11, and go west to 12th Street in the Fairhaven section of Bellingham. Turn left there, south, still on SR 11. Follow it to MP 16, where a left turn (east) will put you on Hiline Road. Reset your odometer to zero at the turn. (Somewhat seasonal waterfalls exist at MP 16.6 and MP 17.3 of SR 11, but parking to view them is a bit tight.)

Hiline quickly becomes gravel surfaced Cleator Road. Look for and park at the upper Fragrance Lake Trailhead, approximately three miles up the steep mountain road. (The lower elevation trailhead is passed when about .8 mile from SR 11.) A snow gate immediately past the upper trailhead is usually open. The road leads to Cyrus Gates Overlook, aka Cleator Overlook, with views westward over Lummi Island and portions of the San Juan archipelago.

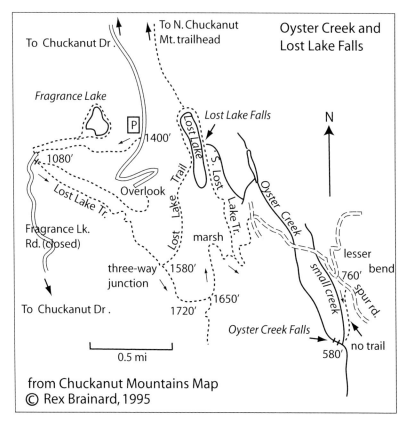

Trail and Falls

The trails for Lost Lake Outlet Falls and Oyster Creek Falls (the following entry) overlap, and can be walked in one longish outing.

The lake's outlet waterfall takes a bit of legwork, but Lost Lake alone is a worthy and popular destination. The narrow lake lies in a trough, pinned against Chuckanut Mountain by a sandstone ridge over a mile in length. Follow the trail downward for 0.75 miles to where it meets the end of Fragrance Lake Road, now closed to all except state park employees. Immediately to the right is the start of the around-the-lake portion of Fragrance Lake Trail. (It is a pleasant three quarters of a mile walk around the lake's shoreline.)

For now, continue down the closed-off road for 0.15 mile to a gated forest road leading left (east). A sturdy sign tags the junction as the start of Lost Lake Trail, with another 2.5 miles to the water. Immediately to the left of the gate a foot trail leaves the road bed and rises to Cyrus Gates Overlook. The Lost Lake road-turned-trail climbs for over a mile and a quarter to a high point of 1580' before arriving at another three-way trail split. Take the signed left branch and, in getting down to Lost Lake level, succeed in losing most of the elevation just gained. When it flattens out, catch glimpses of the water long before arriving at a signed spur trail right (south). It leads to the pretty and remote lake in 0.2 mile. You're not quite to the falls yet, though.

The lake's outlet and falls are found an additional 0.15 mile along the lake's east shore. Follow the obvious trail and stay with it as it veers sharply left (east) away from the lake. It does so to surmount the high sandstone rib which confines the water. The only safe viewing of the fifty-foot *plunge* section of the waterfall is across the narrow outlet and then down the steep escarpment. Mature trees make for good handholds and foot stops.

Oyster Creek Falls

Type of falls:	segmented plunges
Height of falls:	80 feet
Approach:	hike 9.6 miles plus .6 miles no trail
Starting elevation:	1400 feet
Falls elevation:	600 feet
Difficulty:	Strenuous
Seasons for viewing:	S, F, W
Map:	USGS Bellingham South 7.5'

Getting There

Read the *Getting There* section for the previous entry, Lost Lake Outlet Falls. The driving, parking, and trailhead directions are the same. As noted previously, the trails for the pair of entries are partially the same, and the two falls can be seen in one longish trip. See the Trail Map on page 33.

Trail and Falls

Why, you ask, would anyone walk nine and six-tenths miles and then crash through the woods for six-tenths more in order to see a waterfall with a two-and-a-half droplet rating? There is an answer, but first hear some more damaging negativity. Go when the leaves are still hanging on and you will have trouble seeing the drop, even when as close as a hundred feet. Add this: there's a lot of up and down-ness hidden in the above specs. The trail-plus-bushwhack goes more like this: Start at 1400', tramp down to 1080', rise to 1720', drop way down to 600', and then do it all in reverse.

Oyster Creek is special, though, because the waterfall is unexpected. Not to start a gold rush type panic or anything, but few people have ever gone in there. Don't you already yearn to be one of them? There is a true sense of discovery about Oyster Creek Falls. The author located it only because, judging by the topo's contour lines, there *had* to be a waterfall there. You don't fling a creek over a two-hundred-eighty foot escarpment (with a slope of some sixty to seventy degrees) without creating some kind of watery fuss. While the above specs tab the falls at 80 feet in height, that's only the portions that can be seen from its base. How many more plunges there are up there is anybody's guess. Scrambling up the escarpment looks to be doable.

Now for the trail: start by following the *Trail and Falls* description for the previous entry, Lost Lake Outlet Falls. When the three-way junction signed Lost Lake is reached at 2.4 miles and 1580 feet, go right (east) on an unsigned old road. Shortly, cross out of Larrabee State Park land. The way rises gently, turns northward in a saddle at 1720', and soon drops steeply. Keep descending as a trail goes right (south) and upward at 1650' in elevation. Over less than a half mile stretch the route drops some four hundred-twenty vertical feet before leveling out at a marsh 3.3 miles from Cleator Road. 3.6 miles along, three obvious man made routes leave from the north side of a bend, the left-most of which leads to Lost Lake and its outlet falls in about one mile.

Forget Lost Lake for now and keep on keeping on, generally to the east. The 4.1 mile mark presents a four-way intersection of now drivable logging roads. Go straight across. (But look back so you will recognize the back trail on the way out.) The route loses elevation steadily. Cross Oyster Creek at 4.4 miles (900 feet in elevation) and keep on to *Lesser Bend,* 780 feet. The bend, a pronounced switchback, is 4.7 miles from parking.

Note: a rock-toss *west* of the bend the road crosses a small creek which feeds into Oyster Creek at the base of its falls.

Lesser Bend is easy to recognize. The inside of the tight curve is a low rock wall. A spur logging road leads southeasterly downhill off its apex and into a somewhat recent clear cut. The view is open and distant. (On a bearing of 143 degrees lie the distinctive cliffs of the Oyster Dome on Blanchard Mountain, another great hike.)

Walk down the spur road, quite straight for a tenth of a mile. The right hand (west) side of the road pretty much forms the western margin of clear cutting. Where the road bends slightly left in a tenth of a mile, look for a lone western hemlock tree on the right. It is approximately 12 inches in diameter and looks to have been forgotten while all of its mates were falling. Perhaps a pair of pink flagging ribbons still wave directly behind the tree. Regardless, a path through the young alders at that point is plainly visible. But only for a short distance. Keep going when the boot scuffs are lost in thickets of salmonberry, ferns, and planted Douglas firs. Maintain the same general heading and shortly gain the more manageable tread of maturing second growth forest. On a knobby, wooded hump of what is the steep east bank of the noted small tributary, the intrepid will pick up a discernible path leading southward.

If you do not locate a track – with possible remnants of someone's thoughtful flagging – just continue following the creek to the south. The lightly beaten-in path is found anywhere from ten to seventy vertical feet above the small water course. Keep your echo location turned on and eventually the sound of the waterfall will waft upward. It is at that point that the footwork gets tricky. Heading down to the sound is a veritable stumble-jungle of wonderfully healthy sword ferns sporting interwoven, ankle-grabbing fronds. Wait until you come up through it.

Cross the small creek at some point upstream of its confluence with Oyster Creek. The meeting place itself tends to be boggy.

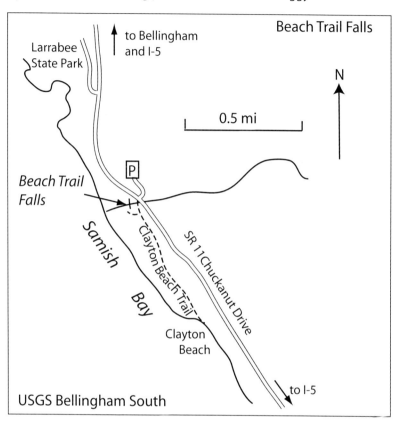

Beach Trail Falls

Type of falls:	Slide
Height of falls:	20 to 25 feet
Approach:	Hike 0.4 mile
Starting elevation:	190 feet
Falls elevation:	130 feet
Difficulty:	Moderate
Seasons for viewing:	Sp, F, W
Map:	USGS Bellingham South 7.5′

Getting There

Coming from the south take I-5 Burlington exit 231, signed Chuckanut Drive and SR 11. Drive north to MP 14.3. From the north, take I-5 exit 250 in Bellingham. Follow Chuckanut Drive or SR 11 signs west and then south to MP 14.3. Park just back from the east side of the highway in a large lot signed for Clayton Beach Trailhead and Fragrance Lake Road.

Trail and Falls

Follow Clayton Beach Trail signs the short distance back out to Chuckanut Drive. Find the trail and a flight of steps on the west side of the highway. Go left at the bottom of the stairway and cross a well-made aluminum footbridge over the unnamed waterfall-bearing creek. Just beyond the south end of the bridge several unsigned as well as un-maintained paths go right (west) into the sparse woods. Stay somewhat near the creek and any of them will lead to the falls, just 0.2 mile from parking.

Clayton Beach Falls is a picturesque slide composed of over-lapping S curves. If you are able to mentally blot out the scars of indiscriminate trampling by the unthinking hordes, it is also a place of contemplative beauty.

San Juan Islands

Unless you have your own boat or aircraft, plus a vehicle stashed on the island of choice, conveyance to at least four of these wondrous isles is by Washington State Ferry from Anacortes. To reach the terminal, leave I-5 at exit 230 in Burlington and drive SR 20 to the west. Where SR 20 turns south for Deception Pass, continue west on Spur 20 to Anacortes. From there follow the ferry signs four miles to the west of downtown.

The only waterfalls in the San Juans are on Orcas Island. Catch an early boat in order to take full advantage of both daylight and a satisfying helping of island mystique. Take a vehicle or at least bicycles aboard the ferry with you.

Cascade Falls

Type of falls:	Slide/Plunge
Height of falls:	40 feet
Approach:	Hike 0.4 mile
Starting elevation:	640 feet
Falls elevation:	505 feet
Difficulty:	Easy
Seasons for viewing:	Sp, F, W
Map:	USGS Mount Constitution 7.5'

Getting There

From the ferry landing on Orcas follow the Horseshoe Highway, the main island thoroughfare, for 8.2 miles north to the town of Eastsound at the head of the horseshoe-shaped island. (Many stores and restaurants.) Go through town to its east edge and to a junction at 9.3 miles, where the route intersects the road to Moran State Park. Turn right (south) and enter the park at 13.5 miles. Drive past park buildings, a campground, and pretty Cascade Lake on your way to a Y junction at 14.9 miles. A left at the fork puts you on the Mount Constitution Road. The Cascade Creek and Falls Trailhead is on the right four tenths of a mile upward, 15.3 miles from the Orcas Island ferry dock.

Trail and Falls

Four waterfalls are found along the creek, three of them scenically viable. All are viewable with an easy walk of 1.4 miles.

Seen from the parking area, there are three paths from which to choose. The center pathway is a connector trail leading south to the Cascade Creek Trail, and this one, simply because it will best tie the four falls together, is the recommended route. In 0.1 mile it reaches the Cascade Creek Trail. (Rustic Falls, not rated but worthy as long as you are there, is directly behind the Cascade Creek Trail sign at the trail junction.)

Go right (west) at the junction, downstream, and reach Cascade Falls in another tenth of a mile. It has both upper and lower viewpoints, easily located.

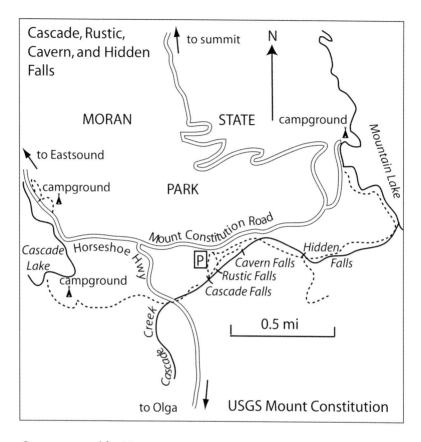

Cascade, Rustic, Cavern, and Hidden Falls

to summit

N

MORAN   STATE   campground

to Eastsound

campground   PARK

Mountain Lake

Mount Constitution Road

Cascade Lake   Horseshoe Hwy

Hidden Falls

P

Cavern Falls

campground

Rustic Falls

Cascade Falls

0.5 mi

Cascade Creek

to Olga   USGS Mount Constitution

Cavern Falls

Type of falls:	Flume/Plunge
Height of falls:	36 feet
Approach:	Hike 0.6 mile
Starting elevation:	640 feet
Falls elevation:	610 feet
Difficulty:	Easy
Seasons for viewing:	Sp, F, W
Map:	USGS Mount Constitution 7.5'

Getting There

Follow the driving directions for Cascade Falls. The trailhead is the same.

Cavern Falls

Trail and Falls

The round-trip to Cavern Falls is only 0.8 mile if Cascade Falls is visited first. Look for Cavern Falls 0.2 mile upstream from the junction of the Cascade Creek Trail and the connector trail from parking. You will hear the falls but will need to get off the trail to have a look. It is composed of a delightful 18-foot descent through a rocky flume which, after a more placid horizontal run of a hundred feet, culminates in a second drop of eighteen feet. Seasonally, the latter might be a plunge or a slide.

Hidden Falls

Type of falls:	Tumble
Height of falls:	15 feet
Approach:	Hike 1.2 miles
Starting elevation:	640 feet
Falls elevation:	710 feet
Difficulty:	Easy
Seasons for viewing:	Sp, F, W
Map:	USGS Mount Constitution 7.5′

Getting There

Follow the driving directions to Cascade Falls. The trailhead is the same. See the Trail Map on page 41.

Trail and Falls

Hidden Falls is only a 1.4 miles round-trip if visits to Cascade and Cavern Falls are included. From the junction of the Cascade Creek Trail and the connector trail from parking, walk upstream (east) past Cavern Falls. Turn right (southeast) when the trail intersects a service road; soon go left when Cascade Creek Trail leaves the service road. Hidden Falls will be found downstream from a footbridge, just steps from the service road and only 0.3 mile upstream from Cavern Falls.

Burlington – Ross Lake Skagit River

Both the Sauk and the Suiattle Rivers are tributaries to the Skagit, but all three are major enough to be treated as independent river valleys. The Skagit River rises in British Columbia, but runs into Washington State's Ross Lake even before it reaches the U.S-Canadian border. All waterfall destinations in the main Skagit River drainage can be reached by driving east from I-5 exit 230 in Burlington. The road is SR 20 as well as the North Cascades Highway. (Exceptions will be noted for the Sauk and Suiattle Rivers.)

Rainbow Falls (Mount Baker)

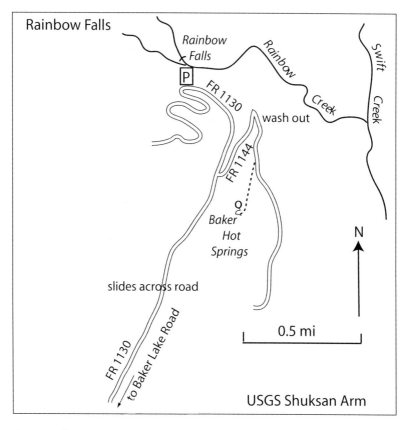

Type of falls:	Plunge
Height of falls:	140 to 150 feet
Approach:	Drive
Falls elevation:	1680 feet
Seasons for viewing:	Sp, Su, F
Map:	USGS Shuksan Arm 7.5'

Getting There

Turn left (north) at MP 82.4 of SR 20 (North Cascades Highway) onto Baker Lake Road. Re-start the mileage count.

At 18.2 miles, just after crossing Boulder Creek via a substantial steel and concrete bridge, turn left (north) on FR 1130. (Note the splendid view of Mount Baker from the bridge.) Once on FR 1130, ignore a left turn onto FR 1131 at 19.8 miles. Pass a bonus flume-like waterfall, about seventy vertical feet of it, at 21.8 miles from SR 20. Pass up FR 1144 on the right at 22.6 miles, and pull into the well-signed parking area for Rainbow Falls in just another tenth of a mile.

The Falls

The viewing rail for Rainbow Falls is only a few feet off the road. Most of the dynamic drop is visible if a little distant from there, but its re-entry into the waiting creek unfortunately cannot be seen. Going beyond the fence in an attempt to see more is definitely ill advised.

A second and smaller "bonus" waterfall is to be found a little more than a mile farther up FR 1130, this one a graceful tumble and slide affair.

Shovel Spur

Type of falls:	Chute
Height of falls:	30 feet
Approach:	Drive
Falls elevation:	430 feet
Seasons for viewing:	Sp, Su, F, W
Map:	USGS Marblemount 7.5′

Getting There

Drive east on SR 20 beyond Marblemount. Park in paved turnouts on the right near MP 114. The correct place is identified by the rock rib through which highway builders blasted for the road. The rib is the same bit of geology responsible for the falls.

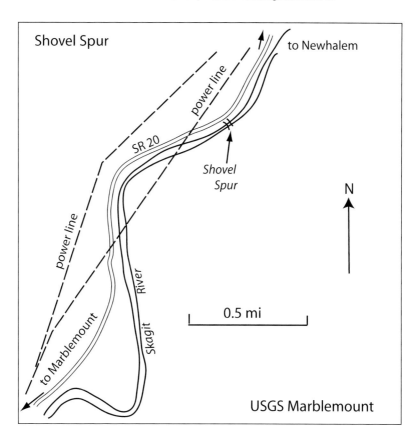

The Falls

Shovel Spur, likely given the name by kayakers who run it regularly, is more a pair of steep rapids than a waterfall. It is better seen at low flow than at high, as lots of water tends to smooth it over. Go down the embankment to connect with the drop's sound and fury.

Newhalem Town Falls

Newhalem Town Falls

Type of falls:	Tumble
Height of falls:	110 to 120 feet
Approach:	Drive
Falls elevation:	520 feet
Seasons for viewing:	Sp, W
Map:	USGS Diablo Dam 7.5'

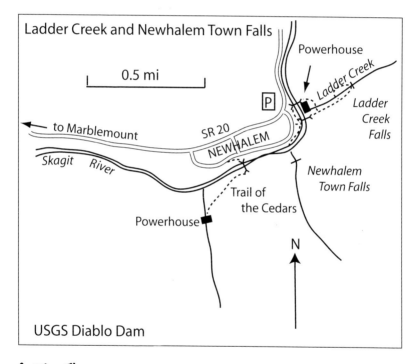

Getting There

Drive SR 20 east from I-5 Burlington exit 230. Continue to MP 120.6 on the east edge of Seattle City Light's employee residential settlement of Newhalem. Park on the right in a large lot signed for Ladder Creek Loop Trail and Gorge Powerhouse. The hydro-generating facility is directly across the Skagit River.

The Falls

Find the paved road leading out of the south end of the parking area. Drive or walk it for less than a tenth of a mile to a close view of the falls across the river. Water that tumbles so far down a steep cliff face has no right to do so unhurriedly, but this one succeeds. If trees are in leaf, find a crude path to river level where views are unobstructed.

Newhalem Town Falls should be visited in the wet season.

Ladder Creek Falls

Type of falls:	Tumble/Plunge, etc.
Height of falls:	60 feet
Approach:	Hike 0.5 mile
Starting elevation:	520 feet
Falls elevation:	720 feet
Difficulty:	Strenuous
Seasons for viewing:	Sp, Su, F, W
Map:	USGS Diablo Dam 7.5'

Getting There

Follow the driving directions for Newhalem Town Falls. Parking is the same. See Trail Map on previous page.

Trail and Falls

The Ladder Creek Loop and Falls Trail is begun by crossing the Skagit River via a dedicated footbridge at the south end of parking. The way, paved at first, leads upward through gardens to the beginning of the loop portion of the route. Go either way.

The three-droplet rating is as much for the whole scenic picture as it is for the falls. And the fall itself is not one but a series of happy events, large and small, which makes the place a joy. Perhaps the centerpiece of this glacier-fed gem is a 60-foot chute and plunge into a deeply incised rock-walled canyon. At its base, the jet of white is momentarily transformed into placid pools of blue-green water before being hurried on down to the Skagit River.

Gorge Creek Falls

Type of falls:	Two-tiered Plunge
Height of falls:	100 feet
Approach:	Drive
Elevation:	1260 feet
Seasons for viewing:	Sp, Su, F, W
Map:	USGS Diablo Dam 7.5'

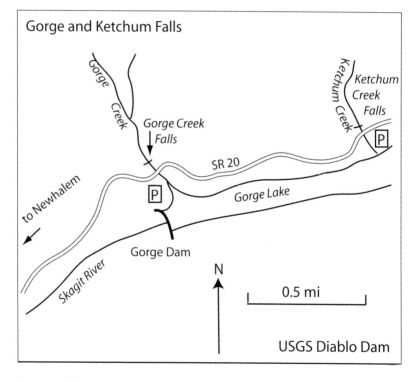

Getting There

Drive east on SR 20 to MP 123.4, well beyond Newhalem. The prominent-ly signed parking area and rest rooms for Gorge Creek Falls are on the right. There is another parking turnout for this popular stop at the east end of the bridge over Gorge Creek.

The Falls

Viewing is from sidewalks on the highway bridge a hundred feet or so over the creek. The falls, in a deep gorge and set back from the bridge, would have a higher rating if closer, and also if the upper tier was not partially obscured by a rock shoulder of its own carving.

Ketchum Creek Falls

Type of falls:	Multiple Plunges
Height of falls:	100 to 110 feet
Approach:	Drive
Elevation:	1360 feet
Seasons for viewing:	Sp, F, W
Map:	USGS Diablo Dam 7.5′

Getting There

Ketchum Creek Falls is 0.9 mile east of Gorge Creek Falls, found at MP 124.4 of SR 20. Park in a turnout just east of the creek crossing on the right (south) side of the highway. See Trail Map on previous page.

The Falls

More modest in most respects than its Gorge Creek counterpart, Ketchum at least offers a better view. Its waters bounce down from the heights close to the north side of the road and keep on going beneath the highway.

John Pierce Falls

Type of falls:	Slide/Tumble
Height of falls:	40 feet
Approach:	Drive
Elevation:	2100 feet
Seasons for viewing:	Sp, Su, F, W
Map:	USGS Ross Lake 7.5′

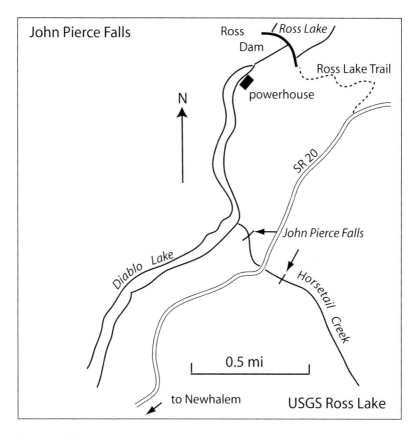

Getting There

Drive SR 20 east to MP 131.9 high above Ross Lake. Park in a turnout on the left (north) side of the highway at the east end of the impressive bridge over Horsetail Creek.

The Falls

Look upstream to see the creek emerge from a deep V at the head of a precipitous canyon. At the bottom of its forty-foot fall the water cavorts away steeply but without fanfare for seven hundred more vertical feet, where it joins the last bit of free-flowing Skagit River within the Cascade Mountains. The USGS map indicates that the waterfall is between the SR 20 bridge and Diablo Lake, but it appears to be right at the bridge. There is so much falling water in sight it's hard to know where this one starts and ends.

Cascade River

Leave I-5 at exit 230 in Burlington and drive east to the town of Marblemount. The route is SR 20 as well as the North Cascades Highway. At MP 106.1 in Marblemount, where SR 20 bends sharply north, leave SR 20 and continue straight east on the Cascade River Road. The route immediately crosses the Skagit River. Zero out your trip meter or note your odometer reading when you leave SR 20.

Get Down Falls

Get-Down Falls

Type of falls:	Flume
Height of falls:	150 feet
Approach:	Drive
Falls elevation:	900 feet
Seasons for viewing:	Sp, F, W
Map:	USGS Big Devil Peak 7.5'

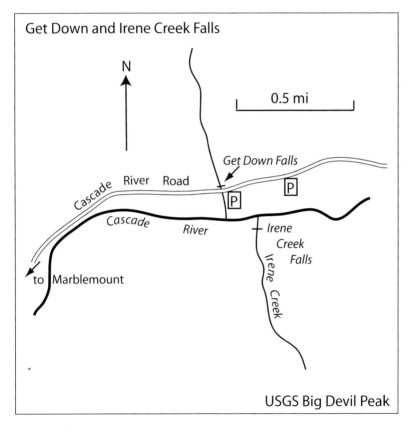

Getting There

Follow the area driving directions under Cascade River (page 54). From its start in Marblemount, drive the Cascade River Road for 5.2 miles. Park along the right side of the road, across from the falls.

The Falls

This pleasant fall slithers and slips a hundred and fifty feet in four increments. The waterfall itself is likely on private property, and it is equally likely that the words "Get Down," painted in green on an adjacent ledge, is a privacy plea, and not really the name of the cataract. At any rate, there is no need to get off the public road to fully enjoy the action.

During high flow, the waterfall's final drop splits into three or more segments.

Irene Creek Falls

Type of falls:	Plunge
Height of falls:	90 to 110 feet
Approach:	Drive
Falls elevation:	800 feet
Seasons for viewing:	Sp, Su, F
Map:	USGS Big Devil Peak 7.5′

Getting There

Follow the area driving directions under Cascade River (page 54). The Irene Creek Falls viewpoint is a half-mile east of Get Down Falls, 5.7 miles along the Cascade River Road. See Trail Map on previous page.

The Falls

This dramatic waterfall and creek enter the Cascade River from the south at 760 feet in elevation. Though the distant view is partially screened by trees, the fall's blaze of white water is easily seen below and somewhat west of the 1,040-foot elevation of the roadway viewpoint. Irene Creek drains a snow bowl of small lakes between Irene Ridge and Razorback Mountain. It runs well most of the summer.

Here are some clues for locating the viewing place: The whole area south of the 5.7 mile mark of Cascade River Road is in recent clear-cut. The best view is from the second of two very short skid roads close to the given mileage, though rapidly growing brush and young hardwood trees are forcing a change. In only a few years there will be no view at all. The second road remnant goes in behind a mound of earth and rock sporting the only standing mature trees on the south side of the road. What the heck; climb the knob if you have to!

So, why not walk down to the river and look across to Irene? The falls would surely be a four-dropper from there except that the route is truly ugly. The innocuous looking clear-cut appears to be a sea of waist high vegetation surrounding young Douglas fir trees. That "sea" is hiding thousands of rotting treetops and other slash that was not picked up after logging. All that bone-breaking stuff serves to hide even more bone-breaking holes and gullies. If a person does struggle that far, the river is still a dangerous twenty-five feet below and the falls view is semi-obscured by trees. The only improvement over the view from the roadway is the music of the falling water.

Fault-Line Falls

Type of falls:	Flume
Height of falls:	30 to 60 feet
Approach:	Drive
Elevation:	1540 feet
Seasons for viewing:	Sp, F
Map:	USGS Sonny Boy Lakes 7.5'

Getting There

Follow the area driving directions under Cascade River (page 54). Locate Fault-Line Falls on the left (north) about a hundred feet before MP 11 of the Cascade River Road.

The Falls

This waterfall is easy to miss. The sizeable ledge that forms its left (west) bank blocks any view from the western approach. Set back in a dark, restful grotto, the creek appears to follow a crack in the earth's crust, geologically referred to as a fault. By whatever name (and more in the judgmental sense of fault-less) four lacy, sliding drops make the place one of quiet beauty. Go and contemplate.

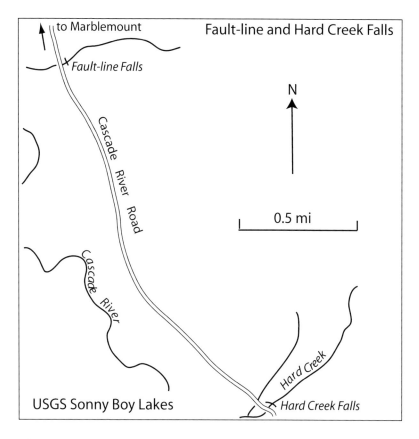

Hard Creek Falls

Type of falls:	Plunge/Tumble
Height of falls:	45 feet
Approach:	Drive
Falls elevation:	1940 feet
Seasons for viewing:	Sp, F
Map:	USGS Sony Boy Lakes 7.5'

Getting There

Follow the area driving directions under Cascade River (page 54). Hard Creek crosses the Cascade River Road at MP 12.8. The creek and low water bridge are signed.

The Falls

Hard Creek Falls itself is uninspiring. Since there are other uplifting reasons for driving the Cascade River Road, stop in on the way by.

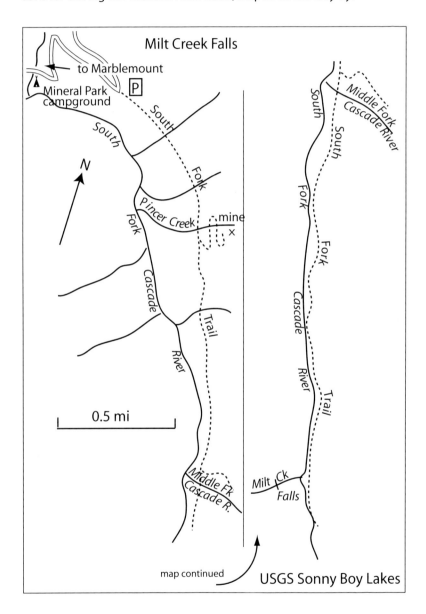

Milt Creek Falls

to Marblemount
P
Mineral Park campground
South
South
N
Fork
Pincer Creek
mine
×
Fork
Cascade
Trail
River
0.5 mi
Middle Fk Cascade R.
South
Middle Fork Cascade River
South
Fork
Fork
Cascade
River
Trail
Milt Ck Falls
map continued
USGS Sonny Boy Lakes

Milt Creek Falls

Type of falls:	Plunge/Tumble
Height of falls:	110 to 115 feet
Approach:	Hike 10.2 miles
Starting elevation:	1680 feet
Falls elevation:	2090 feet
Difficulty:	Strenuous
Seasons for viewing:	Sp, Su, F
Map:	USGS Sonny Boy Lakes 7.5′

Getting There

Follow the area driving directions under Cascade River (page 54). Drive east on Cascade River Road to cross the North Fork Cascade River just short of MP 16. Three switchbacks later (16.7 miles) park at the start of an old road going straight southeast off the tip of a hairpin curve. There are no signs of any sort, but the site is unmistakable.

Trail and Falls

Though the forest road appears to be drivable, washouts and downed trees make it unwise to try. It is maintained as trail only.

At 0.9 mile a rushing creek must be crossed. (In wet seasons, carry old shoes or knee-length rubber boots that far, and stash them in the woods for your return.) Except for small children it is not a dangerous creek to ford. Less than a tenth of a mile after the crossing follow the right fork of a Y in the road. (The left leads to the Spaulding Mine.) The old road gives way to real trail in 1.7 miles. Soon after, glimpsed through a stand of old growth forest, the wild and beautiful South Fork Cascade River comes into view.

At 2.4 miles, and then 2.5 miles, pass twin starts of a trail left (east) up the Middle Fork Cascade River valley, and then cross the sizeable Middle Fork itself via a flattened-off log with no handrail. (At least it's an equally sizeable log.) While on scary subjects, note that the South Fork Trail often sports an inordinate amount of bear scat. Be joyful; make lots of noise, but watch the grunting and snorting sounds.

The trail gradually becomes less used as well as less maintained. There is one area of boulder-sized talus where the route is marked only by small piles of rocks (cairns) that serve as blazes. In a few places where the embankment has been lost to the rampaging river, the trail has gone with it. Most times the detour route is obvious, but in one place it is not. At 4.9 miles the way vanishes altogether. With the river dead ahead and a slide-alder jungle on the left there are only two choices. One is to go home. The other is to backtrack fifteen or twenty feet and, still facing upstream, look left (east) for a faint, boot-trampled way along the edge of the semi-prostrate alder. It soon hooks to the right (south) and leads through a maze of mostly salmonberry bushes to the other side of the one- to two-hundred foot trail washout. Near its end, the correct route heads more toward the river and directly for the flat side of the only large boulder in sight. Go around the boulder's upstream end and easily pick up the trail.

The next physical obstacle is cause for celebration. When a fallen and long dead, can't-miss-sized Douglas fir log blocks the way in a large clearing, climb the steps chain-sawed into its bulk and walk to somewhere near its small end. The trail continues up valley but leave it; the river is visible and the waterfall is roaring its presence. Easily find your own way to water's edge through a sparse community of devil's club and a thin band of trees. Milt Creek Falls is just across the water.

The falls view, broken by a stand of young cottonwoods across the river, would deserve the full five droplets rating if it were less cluttered. For the hardy there is a way. Just upstream, at least until the next flood comes along, a large fallen tree spans the South Fork. One must climb its root ball in order to mount the trunk, and then leave it for a tangle of river debris and growing brush on the other side. The way from there to Milt Creek and its waterfall continues to be rough, but the view is worth it all.

North Fork and Mainstream Sauk River Falls

The North Fork Sauk River comes down out of Dishpan Gap on the Cascade Crest. After joining the Mainstream Sauk, the river flows northward past Darrington and into the Skagit River at Rockport. Waterfalls of the North Fork and Mainstream Sauk are most easily approached from Darrington.

Drive I-5 to Arlington exit 208, and go east on SR 530 to Darrington. Just beyond MP 49, at a T-junction on the east edge of town, leave SR 530 and turn right (south) onto the northern beginning of the Mountain Loop Highway. Record your mileage at the turn.

First Asbestos Falls

ᗜᗜᗜ

Type of falls:	Plunge/Tumble
Height of falls:	360 feet
Approach:	Drive
Falls elevation:	1600 feet
Seasons for viewing:	Sp, F, W
Map:	USGS Helena Ridge 7.5'

Getting There

Follow the area driving directions under North Fork and Mainstream Sauk River (previous page). From the northern beginning of the Mountain Loop Highway in Darrington, drive 2.7 miles south and turn right (west) on unsigned Clear Creek Road, FR 2060. (Clear Creek Campground is almost directly opposite the turn.) At a total of 5.7 miles from Darrington, find ample parking where Asbestos Creek crosses the roadway via a concrete low-water bridge.

Clear Creek Road is quite rough in a few places. While four-wheel drive is not necessary, the route is best driven in a vehicle with high clearance.

The Falls

A fifty-foot section of this many-tiered and lengthy waterfall is downstream of where the creek crosses the access road, but the rest pours from the cliffs to the west. Local folks talk of the place simply as Asbestos Falls, but the USGS Helena Ridge 7.5' topographical map shows only a creek by that name and not the scenic falls. A short distance away, but in Clear Creek, the same map does show an Asbestos Falls. Let the geographers argue the names; the designations 'first' and 'second' are intended only to keep them straight.

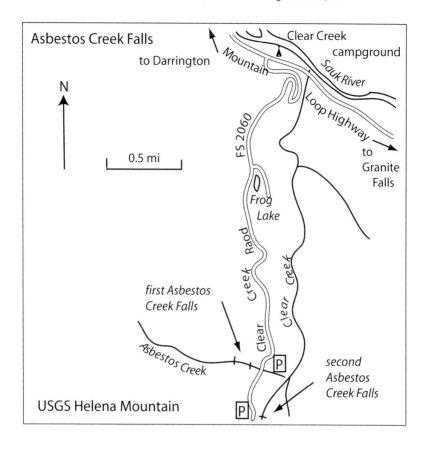

Second Asbestos Falls

Type of falls:	Plunge
Height of falls:	50 feet
Approach:	Walk 0.2 mile, no trail
Starting elevation:	1360 feet
Falls elevation:	1160 feet
Difficulty:	Strenuous
Seasons for viewing:	Sp, F, W
Map:	USGS Helena Creek 7.5'

Getting There

Second Asbestos Falls is not far from First, but following driving directions exactly between the two is critical. Drive onward (south) for three and one-half tenths of a mile from the low-water bridge at First Asbestos Falls. ("One half of a tenth" certainly is awkward language, but odometers don't read in twentieths of miles.) Looking at either this book's area graphic or the USGS Helena Ridge 7.5' topographic map, find the distinctive curve (not a switchback) in Clear Creek Road that bulges eastward. There are small turnouts on the left (east) at the beginning of the bulge and on the left at its apex. Park in either place. The correct curve in the road is in a wooded area. If you pass it up, the road soon breaks out into clear-cut.

Trail and Falls

There is no trail, and though the bushwhack is a bit rough, the waterfall rates four droplets if you catch it in a time of high run-off.

Second Asbestos Falls is in Clear Creek, the main drainage in the area, and is plainly heard from the road. Enter the woods on the left (east) side of FR 2060 at the south end of the distinctive curve. Head generally toward the sound of rushing water, but favor right turns while dodging logs or other impediments. This line will help you avoid the worst brush. It will also nudge you toward the right (south) end of the top of a low cliff which blocks progress if you go directly in from the center point of the bulge. Do not descend the creek's steep embankment. At the right (south) end of the cliff band, go down around to its base and follow left (downstream) beneath the band for about a hundred horizontal feet. Locate a small but fairly obvious and safe ramp of forest floor that leads downward to an 80% unobstructed view of the booming falls. It is very dangerous to attempt improving on this mediocre vantage point.

The viewpoint for Second Asbestos Falls, the only good one, is right on the edge of a potentially deadly drop onto the rocks and into the rushing waters of Clear Creek. Vigilance is the watchword, and that means hanging on to sturdy shrubs.

Second Asbestos Falls

North Fork Sauk Falls

Type of falls:	Chute/Plunge
Height of falls:	75 feet
Approach:	Hike 0.5 mile
Starting elevation:	1400 feet
Falls elevation:	1290 feet
Difficulty:	Moderate
Seasons for viewing:	Sp, Su, F
Map:	USGS Sloan Peak 7.5'

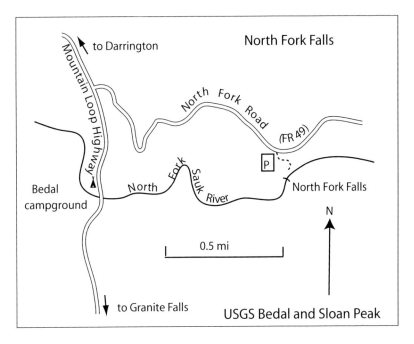

Getting There

Follow the driving directions under North Fork and Mainstream Sauk River (above). Drive south from Darrington on the northern beginning of the Mountain Loop Highway. Pass Clear Creek Road on the right and Clear Creek Campground on the left in 2.7 miles. At 8.6 miles cross to the Sauk River's east bank via a concrete and steel bridge. Stay right (south).

Turn left (east) on FR 49, the North Fork Road, when 16.0 miles from Darrington. Drive a bit over a mile from the turn to signed parking and a trail to the falls.

Trail and Falls

With stairs where needed, a good trail drops gently to an overlook of this literally earth-shaking falls. The awesome dynamic of North Fork Falls is augmented by rock-walls that squeeze the river's contents at the point where bedrock becomes air. Tremendous pressure propels the stream horizontally before surrendering it to gravity. The result is thunderous sound and voluminous spray.

Be careful where you stand to view the action, for there are no warning signs, guardrails or other restraints. A rough, unofficial spur trail leads safely downward to within a few feet of the plunge-pool.

South Fork Sauk River – Monte Cristo

Waterfalls of the South Fork Sauk River are most conveniently accessed by way of the southern beginning of the Mountain Loop Highway in Granite Falls. Leave I-5 at Everett exit 194 and drive east 2.4 miles on US 2. Bear left (northeast) and uphill on SR 204, signed for Lake Stevens. At 4.2 miles go left (north) on SR 9 two more miles to MP 17.6. Turn right (east) onto SR 92 for eight miles to a four-way stop intersection in the middle of Granite Falls. SR 92 ends there, but continue straight east for another half mile to a second four-way stop. A left turn (north) puts you onto the beginning of the Mountain Loop Highway.

The combined campuses of Granite Falls Middle and High Schools are found on the right (east) side of the road shortly after the start of the Mountain Loop Highway.

The South Fork Sauk River begins its journey in the ice and snowfields of the rugged North Cascades. Its three waterfalls are set amid the splendor of historic Monte Cristo, a very real, yet fabled gold and silver mining town of the late nineteenth century. The hitch in hiking to these falls is that one must also factor in the 8.2 round-trip on-foot miles to and from the mining ghost town. The clever among us do it by peddling (and/or pushing) a bicycle to the town site, thereby building in a nearly peddle-free ride out.

Silver and Sunday Falls both depend on seasonal snow melt to be worth viewing. Snowfall in the Monte Cristo region is heavy and the white stuff long lasting, so the possibility of late spring snow avalanches is a point of concern. By the time it is safe to be in there, late June to early July, only about six weeks remain in which to view the falls with an appreciable amount of water going over them. Glacier Basin Falls, on the other hand, also in Monte Cristo Valley, is fed by melt from higher elevation snow and ice field remnants and is scenically viable all summer and fall.

Silver Falls

Type of falls:	Tumble
Height of falls:	80 to 100 feet
Approach:	Hike 11.2 miles
Starting elevation:	2360 feet (at Barlow Pass)
Falls elevation:	3740 feet
Difficulty:	Strenuous
Seasons for viewing:	Su
Maps:	UGS Monte Cristo 7.5', USGS Bedal 7.5'

Getting There

Follow the area driving directions under South Fork Sauk River (previous page). From the southern beginning of the Mountain Loop Highway in Granite Falls, drive 30.4 miles to a large parking area at Barlow Pass. A Northwest Forest Pass is required.

Trail and Falls

Walk or pedal the gated Monte Cristo road with its dilapidated bridges across two channels of the South Fork Sauk River. Don't be too dismayed by the occasional vehicle jouncing by along the way, for the owners of the few cabins at the old mining town-site have gate keys. The very rough road continues on bottomland after the channel crossings and shows ample evidence of periodic flooding. It soon gives way to a series of moderate hills with rest breaks between. The road ends 4.0 miles from parking, where a collapsed vehicle bridge once led across the South Fork Sauk to the town site of Monte Cristo. A good footbridge is in place.

(Bicycles are not permitted beyond road's end or on area trails.) Property owners, too, must walk in, carrying groceries or what-have-you for a bit under two-tenths of a mile to the cluster of rustic summer cabins.

Just before the footbridge comes into view, a left fork of the road leads upward to a campground and to parking for residents. Stay right.

For Silver Falls, cross the river and look for Silver Lake Trail #708 on the right (south) in a couple of hundred feet. The rough trail rises moderately steeply for the additional mile and a half to the falls. On a relatively flat bench on the mountainside, find where the unnamed outlet stream of diminutive Cultus Lake crosses the Silver Lake Trail. Look up to the right (west) at that point to see a ribbon of water splash and plunge from the vertical valley wall. Struggling through thick brush to the base of the waterfall is rewarded only with scratches and ankle twisting, not with improved views.

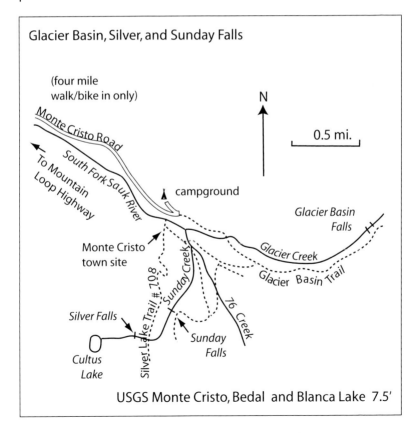

Glacier Basin, Silver, and Sunday Falls

USGS Monte Cristo, Bedal and Blanca Lake 7.5'

Sunday Falls

Type of falls:	Tumble
Height of falls:	120 to 140 feet
Approach:	Hike 8.8 miles
Starting elevation:	2360 feet
Falls elevation:	3300 feet
Difficulty:	Moderate
Seasons for viewing:	Su
Maps:	USGS Monte Cristo7.5', USGS Bedal 7.5'

Getting There

Follow the driving directions under South Fork Sauk River (page 70). From the southern beginning of the Mountain Loop Highway in Granite Falls, drive north and east 30.4 miles to a large parking area at Barlow Pass. A Northwest Forest Pass is required for all vehicles.

Trail and Falls

From Barlow Pass to the footbridge across the Sauk River just below Monte Cristo town site, the walking route is the same as for Silver Falls (see above). Once across the footbridge, at the 4.0-mile point, walk the trail a bit more than a tenth of a mile to the few cabins making up the majority of buildings in the area. Note the rusted, though still operable locomotive turntable to the right of the oval-shaped clearing. This once marked the end of the Everett and Monte Cristo Railroad, focal point of a bustling mining and residential community in the early 1900s.

At the upper (eastern) end of the town site clearing, 4.2 miles from Barlow Pass, note a trail and footbridge to the left (northeast) over 76 Creek, and a second trail right (east) crossing Sunday Creek. A sign points right (east) to Sunday Falls.

Go right, crossing Sunday Creek, and pass along the right side of a cabin signed "76". Bear right past a huge boulder and follow the trail up behind it. Sight a collapsed building in the trees to the left. The timbers are all that remain of the Boston-American Mine's ore concentrator, built in 1917. Due largely to the railroad's failure to survive the onslaughts of the South Fork's rampages, the facility was never used.

At 4.3 miles, go right on old roadway. In another tenth of a mile keep watch on the right for a roughly thirty-foot-diameter clearing on the banks of Sunday Creek. The waterfall is plainly visible upstream during times of high run-off, though hard to see when creek waters are at low flow.

Signs at the site reveal the area was once home to a dance pavilion, as well as the residence of Dr. Marsh, once the town's physician. Time and time again while in this valley, it will be difficult to believe there existed here some half dozen streets, numerous homes and stores, an ill-fated railroad, and three hotels, all built and gone in a relative blink of time.

Glacier Basin Falls

Type of falls:	Tumble/Flume
Height of falls:	60 to 200 feet
Approach:	Hike 10.8 miles
Starting elevation:	2360 feet
Falls elevation:	3500 feet
Difficulty:	Strenuous
Seasons for viewing:	Su, F
Maps:	USGS Monte Cristo 7.5', USGS Bedal 7.5', USGS Blanca Lake 7.5'

Getting There
Follow the area driving directions under South Fork Sauk River (page 70). From the southern beginning of the Mountain Loop Highway in Granite Falls, drive north and then east, for 30.4 miles to a large parking area at Barlow Pass. A Northwest Forest Pass is required for all vehicles.

Trail and Falls
Follow the walking route description (above) for Silver Falls. Once across the footbridge, at 4.0 miles, walk the trail a bit more than a tenth of a mile to the few cabins making up the majority of buildings in the area. At the upper (eastern) end of the clearing, 4.2 miles from Barlow Pass, note a trail and footbridge to the left (northeast) over 76 Creek.

Glacier Basin Falls

Cross the bridge and climb past numerous signs that indicate the size and complexity of this ghost town of a century ago. For openers, this skinny trail was once busy Dumas Street, and it sported a boardwalk thirty-to-forty feet wide. At 4.5 miles, a half-mile from the footbridge over the Sauk, encounter a five-way junction. Left leads to the ruins of the first ore concentrator in the valley, and right goes up to Sunday Flats and Falls. Go straight across the junction onto signed Glacier Basin Trail #719. (The fifth choice, to the right of Glacier Basin Trail, leads to a private cabin.)

In two more tenths of a mile a trail comes up from the left at a sharp angle. This choice presents an alternative for the return trip. It goes down to ford Glacier Creek then joins an historic wagon road back to the campground and footbridge over the Sauk River. For now, continue upward. The way soon reaches tree line. Though the town's first buildings were constructed in this area, snow avalanches destroyed most of them the very first winter. Trees, apparently, have fared no better.

At 5.0 miles, along a stretch from two- to four-tenths of a mile in length, good views of Glacier Basin Falls can be had. Better viewpoints (read that closer) do not exist without climbing the creek bed itself. The top of the waterfall is reached 1.4 miles from the footbridge over the South Fork Sauk River below the town site, 5.4 miles from Barlow Pass.

Goat Lake Outlet Falls

Type of falls:	Tumble
Height of falls:	200 feet
Approach:	Hike 9.5 miles
Starting elevation:	1900 feet
Falls elevation:	3110 feet
Difficulty:	Strenuous
Seasons for viewing:	Su, F
Maps:	Green Trails Sloan Peak #111, 1997 revised edition; or USGS Sloan Peak 7.5' and USGS Bedal 7.5'

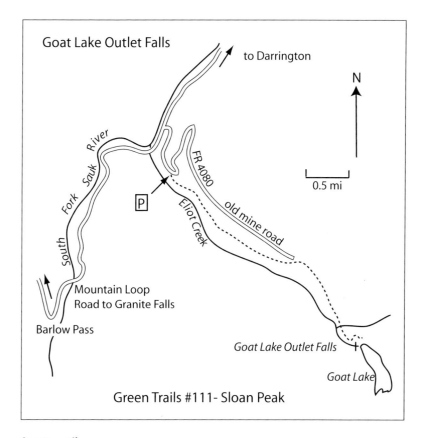

Goat Lake Outlet Falls

to Darrington

N

0.5 mi

South Fork Sauk River

FR 4080

P

Eliot Creek

old mine road

Mountain Loop
Road to Granite Falls

Barlow Pass

Goat Lake Outlet Falls

Goat Lake

Green Trails #111- Sloan Peak

Getting There

Follow the area driving directions under South Fork Sauk River (page 70). Starting at the southern beginning of the Mountain Loop Highway in Granite Falls, drive north and east for 30.4 miles to Barlow Pass. Pavement ends here. Continue on the gravel surfaced Mountain Loop Highway as it swings north toward Darrington. 3.5 miles from Barlow Pass and approximately thirty-four total miles from Granite Falls, turn right (east) on Elliot Creek Road (FR 4080). In 0.9 mile, the road is gated at a signed parking area for Trail #647 to Goat Lake.

Trail and Falls

For many years the trail to Goat Lake was nearly impassable due to swampy terrain, and the only good way to get there was to walk the logging road. That remains an option, but the trail has been relocated and is much more pleasant than treading a road. (The revised Green Trails Sloan Peak map #111, 1997 edition, shows the relocated trail.)

If you do opt for the road, it joins the remains of an historic wagon road, one that once served the hotel and mining town at the lake during the heyday of the Monte Cristo gold and silver rush. At 3.5 miles it intersects Trail #647 and continues to falls and lake.

Find Goat Lake Trail #647 on the south side of the parking area. It begins by angling gently downhill toward Elliot Creek before climbing moderately for most of the remaining distance lake. Not until the last half mile does the way hint of steepness. This waterfall makes no mystery of its whereabouts. It bounces into view from high above the tip of the final switchback before the trail reaches the lake, then splashes happily out of sight far below.

Take careful note of the place where the trail joins the old wagon road. The junction, a left turn on the way out, is easy to by-pass if you haven't taken a backward glance on the way up.

Suiattle River

Leave I-5 at Arlington exit 208 and drive east on SR 530. About fifty-five miles from I-5, and six miles north of Darrington, leave SR 530 and go straight (east) onto Suiattle River Road (FR 26). Restart your mileage count there. The road junction is a scant two-tenths of a mile east of the SR 530 bridge over the Sauk River.

If coming from the north (Mount Vernon area) there is a small mileage advantage in leaving I-5 at Burlington, exit 230, and driving east on SR 20. At MP 97.7 in Rockport, turn right (south) on SR 530 for twelve miles. Suiattle River Road (FR 26) will be on the left (east). Turn left and restart the mileage count.

Suiattle River Road is the main entry route to the northern trails of Glacier Peak Wilderness Area.

Suiattle Falls

This two- to three hundred foot drop from the cliffs of Suiattle Mountain is unrated because it is located a half mile off the north side of FR 26 and in some very rough country. The only reasonably good view of it is found 2.2 miles east of SR 530. Drive slowly in that vicinity, and look for a break in the otherwise solid wall of young alders and birches on your left. The waterfall's stream crosses FR 26 at the site of Lower Suiattle Falls (below).

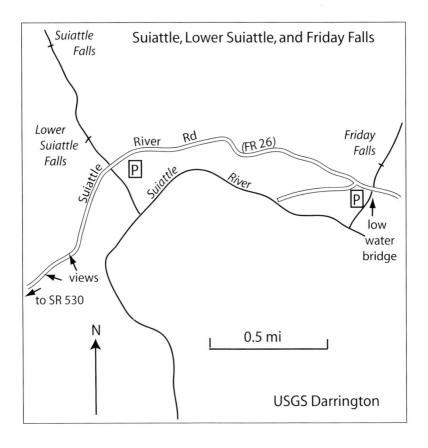

Lower Suiattle Falls

Type of falls:	Flume/Slide
Height of falls:	60 to 70 feet
Approach:	Drive
Falls elevation:	850 feet
Seasons for viewing:	Sp, F, W
Map:	USGS Darrington 7.5'

Getting There

Follow the driving directions under Suiattle River (page 79). Heading east on FR 26, cross the unnamed creek bearing Suiattle and Lower Suiattle Falls at 2.7 miles. Parking for the lower fall is on the right a tenth of a mile beyond the stream crossing.

The Falls

The two-tiered fall is visible from the road, but is more enjoyable after a moderately difficult two-hundred-foot scramble up the creek bed. Above the top tier, another small waterfall is visible, but beyond that the banks steepen and close in on the waterway. Neither the creek bed nor surrounding terrain appears to offer a viable route to the cliffs that birth Suiattle Falls.

A small, unrated, flume-type waterfall appears on the left side of the road three-tenths of a mile east of Lower Suiattle Falls. From even farther east, look back and up toward Suiattle Mountain, where the same creek plummets for hundreds of feet in numerous plunges and tumbles.

Friday Falls

Type of falls:	Tumble/Plunge
Height of falls:	110 to 130 feet
Approach:	Drive
Falls elevation:	800 feet
Seasons for viewing:	Sp, F, W
Map:	USGS Darrington 7.5'

Getting There

Follow the driving directions under Suiattle River (page 79). Friday Falls is found 4.0 miles east of the start of FR 26. There is ample parking on the right (south) side of the road.

The Falls

See Trail Map on page 80. Like Lower Suiattle Falls, Friday Falls may be observed from your vehicle, but the drop occurs about a quarter mile upstream. A route up the east bank, with a rock-hopping crossing over and back again (to avoid a section of washed-out embankment) leads to a view site from atop a prominent and easily climbed boulder.

Teepee Falls

Type of falls:	Flume
Height of falls:	80 feet
Approach:	Drive
Falls elevation:	820 feet
Seasons for viewing:	Sp, Su, F, W
Map:	USGS Prairie Mountain 7.5'

Getting There

Follow the driving directions under Suiattle River. Drive 6.6 miles from the turn onto Suiattle River Road and park on the shoulder just before a high steel bridge over an impressive rock walled canyon.

The Falls

The only safe view of Teepee Falls is from the bridge. While even that flat perspective costs a bunch of superlatives, it is the reason for the low two-drop rating. The canyon itself is awesome.

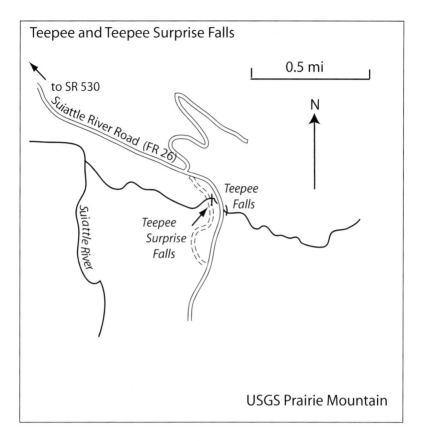

Teepee and Teepee Surprise Falls

0.5 mi

to SR 530

Suiattle River Road (FR 26)

N

Suiattle River

Teepee
Falls

Teepee
Surprise
Falls

USGS Prairie Mountain

Teepee Surprise Falls

Type of falls:	Plunge
Height of falls:	50 feet
Approach:	Walk 0.2 mile
Starting elevation:	870 feet
Falls elevation:	800 feet
Difficulty:	Strenuous
Seasons for viewing:	Sp, Su, F, W
Map:	USGS Prairie Mountain 7.5'

Getting There

Driving and parking directions are the same as for Teepee Falls.

Teepee Surprise Falls

Trail and Falls

The USGS Prairie Mountain 7.5' topographic map shows two waterfall symbols where Teepee Falls is located. With that in mind, and with an ever keen desire to discover new waterfalls, it seemed perfectly natural to search downstream a bit. It was also hoped that a view into the canyon of Teepee Falls would open up.

Find the west end of the guardrail extending back from the bridge over the gorge of Teepee Falls. (The south or downstream side of the road.) Walk sixty-feet back west along the road and look for an unsigned trail through the young cedars. The correct place offers a short climb of the road embankment before dropping steeply to the creek below. The route becomes good trail once on terrain closer to the creek. The gorge runout is reached in about a tenth of a mile.

Views at the lower level, the location of an earlier bridged crossing of this wild creek, are of a pair of drops totaling perhaps only fifty feet, but ones that demonstrate the power of water in a stone-walled prison of its own making. The site is one of crystal-clear waters aglow with the radiance of mossy splendor, truly a place of mystical solitude.

Due to a bend in the creek there is no peering upstream into the awesome gorge of Teepee Falls, but Teepee Surprise is ample reason for the visit.

Gibson Falls

Type of falls:	Flume
Height of falls:	25 to 35 feet
Approach:	Hike 0.6 mile
Starting elevation:	1130 feet
Falls elevation:	1140 feet
Difficulty:	Moderate
Seasons for viewing:	Sp, F
Map:	USGS Huckleberry Mountain 7.5'

Getting There

Follow the driving directions under Suiattle River (page 79). At 9.9 miles east on FR 26 (3.2 miles east of Teepee Falls), turn right (south) on FR 25. It quickly crosses the Suiattle River and trends generally eastward as *South Suiattle River Road*. Ignore an unsigned road just after the signed bridge over Straight Creek. The road narrows before ending at 16.0 miles on the now bridgeless banks of Circle Creek. Park wherever the shoulder is wide enough.

Trail and Falls

Fording Circle Creek can be hazardous, for it often runs fast, deep, and wide and shows few stepping stones. Make sober decisions about your party's ability to cross safely. Knee-high rubber boots may help, but be aware that as little as *fifteen* inches of rushing water can lift most people off their feet. A good safety technique is to walk holding hands in a line parallel to the stream's flow. When one person at a time moves one leg at a time, stability is greatly improved.

Once on the east bank, walk the road up and over a small hill, and then down to a (usually) dry channel at 0.2 mile from Circle Creek. You're almost there, but the final tenth of a mile seems like a long one. The next water that crosses beneath the road by way of a culvert has come over Gibson Falls.

Depending on foliage conditions, the watery action may be somewhat visible upstream from the roadway, but a rather demanding fifty- to seventy-five-foot long bushwhack will show a great deal more. Gibson Falls makes a low-key statement of laughing beauty, a slim, winding thread of silver in a brush-filled grotto. Go up the right (west) bank after skirting a deep roadside pool, the apparent result of an undersized or plugged culvert. Persevere, knowing that few before you will have ventured off the road.

Arlington - Darrington

Waterfalls of the North Fork Stillaguamish are best accessed via I-5 Arlington exit 208. The road, SR 530, runs through Arlington city center to Darrington, where it abruptly turns north toward the North Cascades Highway at Rockport. A right turn (south) at that same junction is onto the northern beginning of the Mountain Loop Highway.

The North and South Forks of the Stillaguamish River are not only very different in character but are widely separated geographically as well. With the book's underlying premise of driving convenience in mind, the numerous waterfalls of the South Fork 'Stilly' will be found in the section entitled Granite Falls, South Fork Stillaguamish River.

North Fork Stillaguamish River

Boulder Falls

Type of falls:	Tumble
Height of falls:	50 to 70 feet
Approach:	Hike 1.2 miles plus 0.3 mile no trail
Starting elevation:	1000 feet
Falls elevation:	880 feet
Difficulty:	Strenuous
Seasons for viewing:	Sp, Su, F, W
Maps:	USGS Mount Higgins 7.5,
	USGS Meadow Mountain 7.5'

Getting There

Leave I-5 at Arlington exit 208, and drive east on SR 530. Turn right (south) on French Creek Road immediately west of MP 41. Ignore all side roads. Parking for the Boulder River Trail, road's end, is in 3.7 miles. The parking area is poorly designed and is much too small for a popular trail. Park facing out, and try to position your vehicle to avoid being blocked by another.

Trail and Falls

The trail uses an abandoned logging roadway and is totally flat to the turnoff for Boulder Falls. Pass beneath rock walls on the left (east) at 0.6 mile. In the long ago a void in the precipitous terrain at the base of the cliffs was bridged with old growth logs, a couple of which are slumping badly. (It's fine for foot traffic, but don't try it with your big rig.) Just beyond the vertical rock look for a couple of unsigned routes on the right (west) leading steeply down to Boulder River. The second of these might be a slightly better choice, but both are steep and on loose, rocky ground. Though Boulder River runs generally south to north, its falls are on a tenth of a mile stretch heading nearly due east. You will be looking upstream on your approach. The tricky part of this exercise is in finding a decent spot from which to see the action once there.

If you don't see those unofficial routes, and the Boulder River Trail has jogged right and started uphill for the first time, you have passed the un-marked turn-offs by about a tenth of a mile.

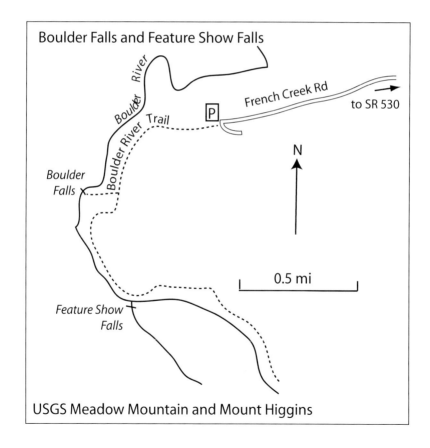

Boulder Falls and Feature Show Falls

USGS Meadow Mountain and Mount Higgins

Feature Show Falls

Feature Show Falls

Type of falls:	Slide/Veil
Height of falls:	110 feet
Approach:	Hike 2.5 miles
Starting elevation:	1000 feet
Falls elevation:	1180 feet
Difficulty:	Moderate
Seasons for viewing:	Sp, Su, F, W
Maps:	USGS Mount Higgins 7.5',
	USGS Meadow Mountain 7.5'

Getting There

Follow the driving and walking directions for Boulder Falls. Feature Show Falls is on the same Boulder River Trail. See Trail Map on page 89.

Trail and Falls

Boulder River is audible even from the trailhead, but it becomes a full roar at the base of infamous Granny Grunt Hill, 0.7 mile in. (Okay, it's neither detestable nor very high.) Old road gives way to forest trail soon after the hill is topped, and the never-to-be-cut old growth forest of Boulder River Wilderness Area begins. The route is all humps and bumps for the remainder of the way.

A pretty waterfall hisses down the cliffs forming the west bank of the river at 1.2 miles, but this one is only a teaser. Call it Preview Falls. The real attraction, a bit farther on, leaves no doubt about which one you have come to see. The water of an unnamed creek plunging down Mount Ditney's northeastern flank appears to pause on the brink. Grand entrance? It then swirls over the edge to dash against a cleaver, splitting itself into a pair of racing jets. These divide and subdivide to form a lacy veil that weaves its way unhurriedly down the wall. There is no run-out for Feature Show Falls; it drops climactically into the rapids of Boulder River. This waterfall is aptly named, for a different show is playing each time you go there. Feature Show has the power to mesmerize.

A third waterfall in the style of Feature Show Falls, though certainly without its magnificence, occurs another mile upstream.

Granite Falls

Granite Falls
South Fork
Stillaguamish River

The wild South Fork Stillaguamish, unlike its North Fork cohort, isn't the least bit stingy with its magic of falling water. The river's remote canyon was once the route of the legendary Monte Cristo Railroad, so it is also a place brimming with history. Granite Falls – the town – is truly the gateway to the waterfalls (and a whole lot more) of the South Fork Stillaguamish River.

Reach the town of Granite Falls by leaving I-5 at Everett exit 194 and driving east for a little over two miles on US 2. Bear left and uphill onto SR 204, signed for Lake Stevens. When SR 204 reaches SR 9 at 4.4 miles, follow SR 9 north to MP 17.6 and turn right (east) onto SR 92. The state designation officially ends in another eight miles at a four-way stop in the center of Granite Falls. Proceed straight east on East Stanley Street to a second four-way intersection about 15 miles from I-5.

A left turn here (north) is onto the southern beginning of the Mountain Loop Highway. Though the "loop" starts out northward, it soon runs some thirty miles east along the South Fork Stillaguamish River to Barlow Pass. There, site of the gated four-mile walking road into gold era Monte Cristo, good pavement ends, and the gravel surfaced Mountain Loop heads north another twenty-five miles to intersect SR 530 in Darrington.

Reset your mileage at the start of the Mountain Loop Highway. For all waterfalls in the South Fork system mileages will be given from this southern beginning of the Mountain Loop Highway. To be certain you are at the correct four-way intersection, note that the road soon passes the combined campuses of Granite Falls Middle and High Schools.

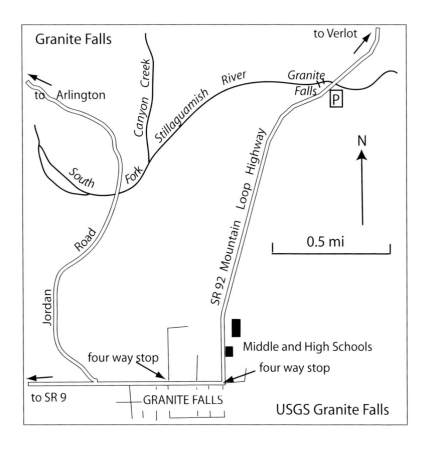

Granite Falls

Type of falls:	Tumble
Height of falls:	30 to 50 feet
Approach:	Walk 0.3 mile
Starting elevation:	380 feet
Falls elevation:	260 feet
Difficulty:	Moderate
Seasons for viewing:	Sp, Su, F, W
Map:	USGS Granite Falls 7.5′

Getting There

Follow the area driving directions from I-5 under South Fork Stillaguamish River (page 93). Drive 1.4 miles north on the Mountain Loop Highway. Park on the left before the bridge which spans the deep canyon of the South Fork.

Trail and Falls

Walk the gravel-surfaced path leading down to the series of falls. A long fishway and tunnel have been constructed to allow salmon to bypass the cascade and to reach spawning beds up river. The public is free to walk atop the steel-grate over the fishway.

The popularity of Granite Falls has as much to do with its deeply sculpted canyon as with its falling waters. Look upstream; the entire river is squeezed between narrowing walls of rock. While continuing its descent it threads a dashing course through carved channels and over smooth ledges on its way past a lengthy viewing area. There is much to see and think about here.

First Falls

Type of falls:	Slide
Height of falls:	35 feet
Approach:	Drive
Falls elevation:	1000 feet
Seasons for viewing:	Sp, Su, F, W
Map:	USGS Verlot 7.5'

Getting There

Follow the area driving directions under South Fork Stillaguamish River. From the beginning in of the Mountain Loop Highway in the town of Granite Falls, drive 11.8 miles north and east. Turn right (south) on Mount Pilchuck Road. (The turn is soon after the crossing of a highway bridge over the South Fork Stillaguamish River, and about one mile east of the Verlot Public Service Center.) Turn right again (west) onto FR 4201 after only a fourth of a mile. Park at the falls in another four-tenths of a mile, 12.4 total miles from the start of the Mountain Loop Highway.

The Falls

The waters of an unnamed creek cascade from cliffs adjacent to the south side of FR 4201. Unpoliced partying and general overuse of this site are responsible for a portion of the waterfall's low rating.

Heather Creek Falls

Type of falls:	Tumble
Height of falls:	50 to 90 feet
Approach:	Walk 0.2 mile, 0.1 no trail
Starting elevation:	980 feet
Falls elevation:	1020 feet
Difficulty:	Strenuous
Seasons for viewing:	Sp, Su, F, W
Map:	USGS Verlot 7.5'

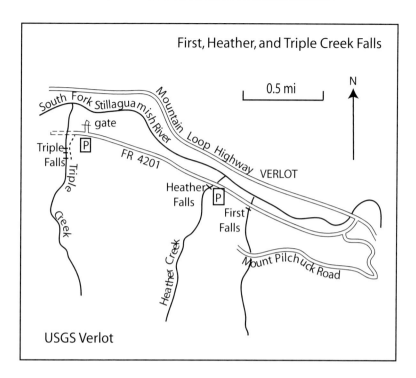

First, Heather, and Triple Creek Falls

0.5 mi

N

South Fork Stillaguamish River

Mountain Loop Highway

gate

Triple Falls

Triple Creek

FR 4201

VERLOT

Heather Falls

First Falls

Heather Creek

Mount Pilchuck Road

USGS Verlot

Getting There

Follow the area driving directions under South Fork Stillaguamish River and those for First Falls (above). Heather Creek Falls is 0.9 mile from the start of FR 4201, and a half-mile beyond parking for First Falls.

Watch closely for an unsigned road remnant on the left (south). Immediately to the right (west) of the vague road remnant is what appears to be a tiny pond, but the pool is in fact a placid section of Heather Creek. Park on the road shoulder.

Trail and Falls

To catch glimpses of the waterfall from FR 4201, walk or drive a short distance farther and look left through the trees. A direct approach to the cataract from where it is partially visible along the road would be tough due to one or more creek crossings coupled with intervening bogs. The best way in is a short but demanding trail-less route starting from the end of the short road remnant beside the creek. The trail-less route itself is little more than a hundred fifty feet long, but is filled with deep gullies, braided channels of the main creek, and multiple layers of moss-be-decked fallen trees. On the other hand, don't let anything described here actually *discourage* you.

Triple Creek Falls
🝰🝰🝰

Type of falls:	Flume/Plunge
Height of falls:	10 to 40 feet
Approach:	Walk 0.4 mile
Starting elevation:	940 feet
Falls elevation:	990 feet
Difficulty:	Moderate
Seasons for viewing:	Sp, Su, F, W
Map:	USGS Verlot 7.5'

Getting There
Follow the area driving directions under South Fork Stillaguamish River, also those for First Falls (previous page). Triple Creek Falls is accessed from the end of the drivable portion of FR 4201, approximately 1.6 miles west of First Falls. The road becomes increasingly less vehicle friendly nearing its end; a good stopping place is near a gated side road on the right (north) at that 1.6 mile point.

Trail and Falls
There is no sanctioned trail to Triple Creek Falls, but there are good im-promptu paths. Walk the remains of FR 4201 west from parking for 0.1 mile to where it is choked by fallen tree debris. (If the branches have been removed, the old road runs right through Triple Creek very shortly be-yond.) Look for several scuff-trails up the ten-foot left (south) embank-ment and climb one of them. The hardest part is over, and the second tenth of a mile of unofficial trail to the first flume-like drop is easy to lo-cate. Two more sections of waterfall are found upstream from the first one, though the trail does become rough and steep. The uppermost fall is about thirty-five feet in height. If more falls call out to you, they're likely waiting up above.

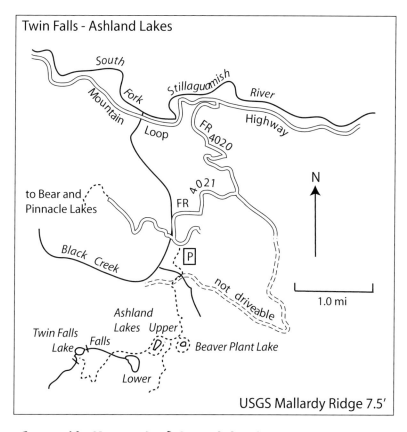

Twin Falls - Ashland Lakes

Type of falls:	Plunge/Tumble
Height of falls:	120 feet
Approach:	Hike 9.4 miles
Starting elevation:	2320 feet
Falls elevation:	2350 feet
Low point:	2140 feet (on trail)
High point:	2846 feet (on trail)
Difficulty:	Strenuous
Seasons for viewing:	Su, F
Maps:	Green Trails Silverton #110, USGS Malardy Ridge 7.5'

Trail to Twin Falls – Ashland Lakes

Getting There

Follow the area driving directions under South Fork Stillaguamish River. Drive north and east on the Mountain Loop Highway from the town of Granite Falls. At 15.6 miles turn right (south) onto FR 4020, signed for Ashland, Bear, and Pinnacle Lakes. Follow Ashland Lakes Trailhead signs for all route changes described below.

Re-start the mileage count at the beginning of FR 4020. After 2.5 miles turn right (west) on FR 4021 and continue to the 3.8-mile mark. Go left there (southeast) and uphill somewhat steeply on an unsigned and narrow crushed rock road, but for only two-tenths of a mile farther. Parking and road's end is just beyond the large DNR Ashland Lakes trailhead sign.

Trail and Falls

Adding "Ashland Lakes" to the title above is intended to distinguish this entry from another Twin Falls on the South Fork Snoqualmie River.

Walk nearly level old road for 0.5 mile to a king-sized park bench (chain sawed from a fallen log) and cross a branch of Black Creek on a good footbridge. At 0.7 mile, where the old road continues straight ahead on its way to Bear and Pinnacle Lakes, turn left and uphill (south) on a short road spur. At the top of the hill, 0.8 mile, a cleared area signals the start of forested trail. Pass a left-leading trail to Beaver Plant Lake at 1.5 miles, and take the right tine of a trail fork to Upper Ashland Lake at 1.8 miles. (Left at the fork leads to the summit of Bald Mountain.)

Upper Ashland Lake, the high elevation point of the hike at 2,846 feet, is reached at approximately the 2.0-mile mark. Take the right fork of a trail split and go by way of the lake's north shore. The choice is slightly longer, but the way is clad almost entirely with doubled boardwalk planking. (It is also far less slippery than the trail along the south shore.) In addition to sporting flown-in toilets, the north shore route also avoids a bridge-out situation at the lake's west outlet end. Nearing the outlet from the north, watch for a right turn (west) to start the descent to Lower Ashland Lake.

Lower Ashland's outlet end is 2.8 miles into the hike. At a fork there, a route to the left crosses the outlet creek to campsites and another pit toilet. The right leg continues the long downward trend toward Twin Falls Lake. The trail is ragged and often muddy. From a deep ravine, below and off to the right, at about 4.5 total miles, you will begin to hear and see bits of 400-foot Lower Twin Falls. Be happy with these thin slices, though, for anything closer becomes extremely dangerous. Take heart; the safe and more picturesque waterfall is not far off. After a rough and rocky stream crossing, at 2,140 feet, the trail climbs to Twin Falls Lake at 4.7 miles from parking. Several falls viewpoints will be found along the west shore of the pretty lake.

Good DNR signage tells the impressive geologic story of Twin Fall's origin during the ice age of 12,000-plus years ago.

Perry Creek Falls

Type of falls:	Plunge
Height of falls:	50 to 70 feet
Approach:	Hike 4.0 miles
Starting elevation:	2100 feet
Falls elevation:	3360 feet
Difficulty:	Moderate
Seasons for viewing:	Sp, Su, F
Maps:	Green Trails Monte Cristo #143, USGS Bedal 7.5'

Getting There

Follow the area driving directions under South Fork Stillaguamish River. At 25.3 miles of the Mountain Loop Highway, pass the Big Four Ice Caves Picnic Area on the right. Less than a mile east of there, 26.0 miles from the start of the "Loop" in Granite Falls, turn left (north) on FR 4063. Ignore a right turn about a half mile in, and park at the Mount Forgotten trailhead at road's end, one mile from Mountain Loop Highway.

Note: Vehicle space at this popular trail consists of single-file, parallel parking solely on the road's west shoulder. The only turn-around is in the road bed itself. Turn your vehicle to face out, or risk backing up a long way at the end of the hike.

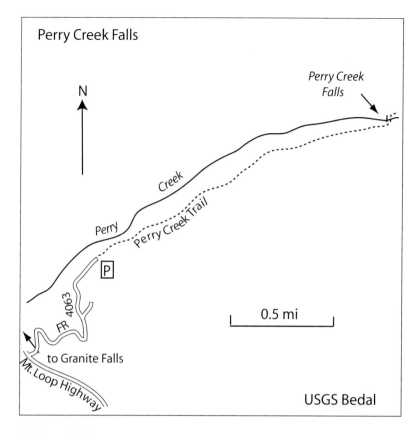

Trail and Falls

The trail rises moderately all the way to the falls. As openings in tree cover permit, look west across Perry Creek Valley to see a couple of long – and seasonal – waterfalls. They are too distant, unfortunately, to stand the scenic viability test for inclusion here.

There is little chance of bypassing Perry Creek Falls, for at the 2.0-mile point the trail comes very close to where the creek flings its contents into a deep abyss. A much better view can be had with a somewhat strenuous climb down the west bank. Get there by continuing up Mount Forgotten Trail a short distance to a sometimes wet fording of Perry Creek. Go left after the crossing to find the most skid-proof way downstream on the west bank's steep slope. The descent is not dangerous, but the gorge lip adjacent to it is certainly perilous.

Twentytwo Creek Falls

The Falls of Twentytwo Creek

Follow the area driving directions under South Fork Stillaguamish River. Drive the Mountain Loop Highway north then east from the town of Granite Falls. At 12.8 miles from the four-way stop on the east edge of town turn right (south) into the signed parking area for Lake Twentytwo Trail.

Twentytwo Creek, which runs directly and precipitously to the South Fork Stillaguamish River, is unique among waterfall-bearing streams. In less than two map miles, beginning as the outlet for beautiful Lake Twentytwo, the waterway drops fourteen hundred feet to join the South Fork. Those numbers spell w-a-t-e-r-f-a-l-l-s. There are six keepers in that stretch. One more, too seasonal to be rated, is found on an unnamed watercourse parallel to Twentytwo Creek. All are located within a relative few feet of Lake Twentytwo Trail.

Only one among the cluster of waterfalls has an official name. Giving out so many new titles would be to take something away from them. Since it is more important to point out where they can be found, the silvery drops will be referred to by their positions along the trail. Or call them all Wonderful.

The lower portion of trail passes through an old growth forest set aside in 1947 by order of the U.S. Secretary of Agriculture. In a spirit ahead of its time, the Forest Service sought to protect a largely undisturbed block of pristine forest as a study area, 790 acres of it. The intent was to later compare its plant and animal populations to those of lands under more "intensive" management. (Sounds a little like clear cutting, doesn't it?) No such studies seem ever to have been conducted, but the preserve exists still.

Since Lake Twentytwo itself is only 0.3-mile beyond the last of six waterfalls, why not go the distance? The lake was formed by the scooping and grinding action of countless tons of glacial ice bearing down from the heights. Even now, snow build-up at the base of cliffs across the lake often develops minor ice caves, similar to those accessible from Big Four Picnic Area.

It is common through winter to find snow at or below Fifth Falls, and to find two to three feet of it at the lake. But so many people make the trek year round that nearly always there is a boot-beaten path to the goal.

Twentytwo Creek Falls

Type of falls:	Tumble/Plunge
Height of falls:	15 to 50 feet
Approach:	Hike 1.4 miles
Starting elevation:	1040 feet
Falls elevation:	1340 feet
Difficulty:	Moderate
Seasons for viewing:	Sp, Su, F, W
Map:	USGS Verlot 7.5'

Getting There

Find the driving directions under the section heading above, The Falls of Twentytwo Creek.

Trail and Falls

A bonus waterfall, i.e., unrated, can be heard from parking if you happen to be there during a time of high runoff. The falling water, of two-droplet proportions and a fifty- to seventy-foot tumble, is easily seen to the left of the trail about two hundred feet from parking.

The trail rises only moderately while nearly paralleling both the highway and the South Fork Stillaguamish River. It climbs its way westward through preserved old growth forest. In 0.7 mile the trail crosses a footbridge over Twentytwo Creek, directly astride Twentytwo Creek Falls.

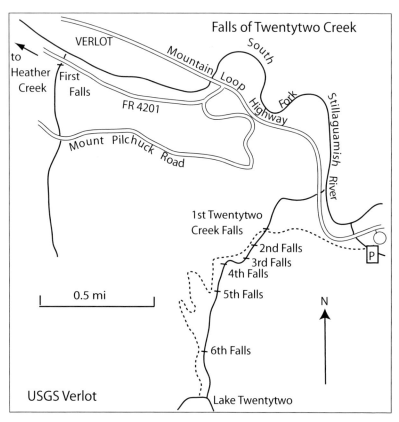

Second Twentytwo Creek Falls

Type of falls:	Tumble/Plunge
Height of falls:	30 feet
Approach:	Hike 1.8 miles
Starting elevation:	1080 feet
Falls elevation:	1460 feet
Difficulty:	Moderate

Seasons for viewing:	Sp, Su, F, W
Map:	USGS Verlot 7.5'

Getting There

Follow the driving directions under The Falls of Twentytwo Creek.

Trail and Falls

Second Twentytwo Creek Falls is 0.2 mile up trail from Twentytwo Creek Falls. Once across the bridge the trail swings sharply south and more or less parallels the stream upward. Second Falls may be seen a short distance to the left off a switchback.

Third Twentytwo Creek Falls

This potentially spectacular drop is unrated due to poor and dangerous viewing. It thunders downward some one hundred-fifty feet, but is deeply incised in a hidden rocky cleft. The same mass of bedrock that requires the trail to switchback right at this point also blocks any chance of seeing the drop either safely or well. The only safe view of Third Falls is from a few steps off the trail. Hear its throaty voice at 1,620 feet in elevation, only two-tenths of a mile upstream from Second Falls.

Fourth Twentytwo Creek Falls

Type of falls:	Tumble/Plunge
Height of falls:	70 feet
Approach:	Hike 2.6 miles
Starting elevation:	1080 feet
Falls elevation:	1640 feet
Difficulty:	Moderate
Seasons for viewing:	Sp, Su, F, W
Map:	USGS Verlot 7.5'

Getting There

Follow the driving directions under The Falls of Twentytwo Creek.

Trail and Falls

Just two-tenths of a mile upstream from Third Falls, look off to the left for number four. A short trail leads off the apex of yet another switchback, and leads steeply and roughly down to good views. A third tier of the same series of drops can be seen another tenth of a mile upward, again on the left.

Fifth Twentytwo Creek Falls

Type of falls:	Tumble/Plunge
Height of falls:	130 to 150 feet
Approach:	Hike 3.8 miles
Starting elevation:	1080 feet
Falls elevation:	1880 feet
Difficulty:	Strenuous
Seasons for viewing:	Sp, Su, F, W
Map:	USGS Verlot 7.5'

Getting There

Follow the driving directions under The Falls of Twentytwo Creek.

Trail and Falls

Note that the difficulty rating has changed from "Moderate" for earlier waterfalls on Lake Twentytwo Trail to "Strenuous". The higher one climbs, the more rocky, root-filled, and muddy the trail becomes. Don't be deterred, for Fifth Falls has a three-droplet rating and Sixth Falls has been given a four.

After Fourth Falls, Lake Twentytwo trail climbs westward away from the creek for a half mile before returning once more to parallel the dynamic stream. Listen for Fifth Falls when 0.5 mile upward from Fourth Falls, and look left for it within a tenth of a mile more. Just beyond Fifth Falls the trail enters a distinctive clearing where it switchbacks up and then across the top of an old talus slope, or boulder field.

Fifth Falls is sometimes segmented, and its left-most run disappears in dryer seasons.

Sixth Twentytwo Creek Falls

Sixth Twentytwo Creek Falls

Type of falls:	Tumble/Veil
Height of falls:	70 feet
Approach:	Hike 5.2 miles
Starting elevation:	1080 feet
Falls elevation:	2300 feet
Difficulty:	Strenuous
Seasons for viewing:	Sp, Su, F, and W
Map:	USGS Verlot 7.5'

Getting There

Follow the driving directions under The Falls of Twentytwo Creek.

Trail and Falls

After ascending the open talus slope above Fifth Falls the rocky trail re-enters the forest. It rises for another two-tenths of a mile before beginning to level out. When Twentytwo Creek again appears on the left (east) side of the trail, be on the lookout for flashes of silver in that direction. This picturesque drop is not marked by any identifiable change in the trail, but the above combination of circumstances makes it easy to find.

Good views of this pretty attraction require about fifty feet of trail-less brush-grabbing, but any four-droplet waterfall is worth it.

Everett-Stevens Pass

The Stevens Pass Highway, US Route 2, begins in Everett at I-5 exit 194 and climbs over the Cascade Mountains to eastern Washington. For much of its way to the summit it follows the mainstream and South Forks of the Skykomish River. Namewise, the Skykomish has been shortchanged. It doesn't receive individual recognition until the more mountainous Tye and Foss Rivers combine near the town of Skykomish. Only forty-five miles downstream miles later it is forced to surrender its identity by blending with the Snohomish River.

The north and south branches of the Skykomish River each figure prominently in the history of Washington State. Its South Fork headwaters in Stevens Pass as the Tye River, and is the route of the state's first cross-Cascades railway. For centuries unknown, its remote North Fork was the major trade route for Native Americans trekking from Puget Sound villages to eastern Washington. In territorial days settlers used the same cross-mountain trail, and it remains a popular backpacking route to the present day. In 1889, gold prospecting up the North Fork Skykomish River led to ore discoveries in fascinating Monte Cristo.

Leave I-5 at Everett exit 194. Drive east on US 2, the Stevens Pass Highway. Driving directions for the waterfalls of both forks of the Skykomish and their tributaries begin with mileage points along US 2.

Mainstream and South Fork Skykomish River

Explorer Falls

Type of falls:	Plunge
Height of falls:	90 feet
Approach:	Hike 2.6 miles
Starting elevation:	600 feet
Falls elevation:	880 feet
Difficulty:	Easy
Seasons for viewing:	Sp, F, W
Map:	USGS Lake Chaplain 7.5′

Getting There

In Monroe, turn north off US 2 onto Woods Creek Road. The turn (a left if approaching from Everett) is about mid-way of the city's long downtown section. The road splits at 10.4 miles from US 2. Go right (still north) on Lake Roesiger Road. In another fraction of a mile the lake road confusingly splits into North and South forks. (Each road runs north, but along different sides of the water.) Take the right turn onto *South* Lake Roesiger Road. Yup; sounds totally illogical. 12.7 miles from Monroe turn right (east) onto Monroe Camp Road. The turn is opposite the Lake Roesiger Store.

Drive east on Monroe Camp Road past Camp Brinkley, the Boy Scout Cascade Reservation, in a bit over one mile. At 14.0 miles the pavement ends. Park where the road is gated 15.0 total miles from US 2 in Monroe.

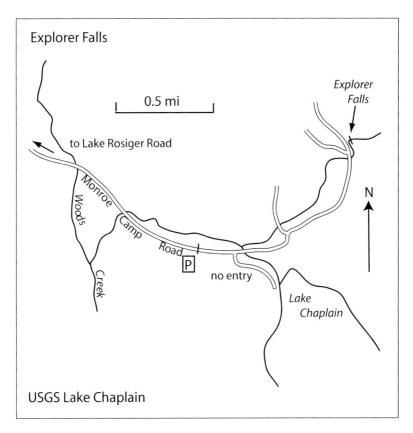

Explorer Falls

0.5 mi

to Lake Rosiger Road

Monroe Camp Road

Woods

Creek

P

no entry

Explorer Falls

N

Lake Chaplain

USGS Lake Chaplain

Trail and Falls

Beyond the gate the road drops gently to cross a wetland. Then, just as gently, it rises for the remaining mile to the waterfall. Along the way it passes the gated entrance (right) to the Lake Chaplain Reservoir. Take the right fork at a road choice, 1.2 miles, and look ahead to a noticeable stand of mature Douglas fir trees on the right. Immediately beyond them, also on the right, is a short road remnant ending in a path which leads to a creek. Explorer Falls is about one hundred-fifty feet upstream from there. Although an abused and washed out trail leads to glimpses from the top of the waterfall, the best views are obtained by rock hopping and scrambling up the streambed to the fall's base.

The top-view trail starts a bit downstream from where you first reach the creek and is on the opposite bank.

Olney Falls

Type of falls:	Plunge/Tumble
Height of falls:	75 to 100 feet
Approach:	Hike 3.4 miles
Starting elevation:	200 feet
Falls elevation:	240 feet
Difficulty:	Moderate
Seasons for viewing:	Sp, F, W
Map:	USGS Wallace Lake 7.5′

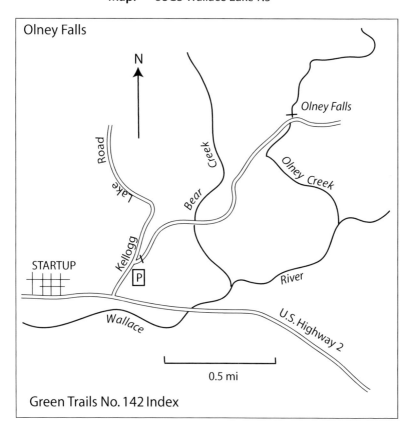

Olney Falls

Green Trails No. 142 Index

Getting There

Leave I-5 at Everett exit 194 and drive to the east edge of the town of Startup. Turn left there (north) on Kellogg Lake Road. In only 0.2 mile, park on the right shoulder near a gated forest road. Take care not to block the road entrance. Towing is almost a certainty if you do.

Trail and Falls

The forest road is in a somewhat recent clear-cut all the way to Olney Falls. In 0.3-mile, cross Bear Creek and start uphill to cross a ridge at 280 feet in elevation. Power lines at the same point represent the 1.3-mile mark. Olney Creek and Falls soon announce themselves as the road crosses a sturdy bridge over a rugged canyon, 1.7 miles from Kellogg Lake Road.

The cataract is just upstream. The wide spread of the seventy-five to one hundred foot vertical drop is due to seasonal fluctuations in stream flow. Olney Creek drains a block of country that holds its snow cover well into June, but the waterfall is often unimpressive through the summer months.

Lake Isabel Outlet Falls

Type of falls:	Tumble/Slide
Height of falls:	200 to 240 feet
Approach:	Hike 7.0 miles
Starting elevation:	560 feet
Falls elevation:	2820 feet
Difficulty:	Strenuous
Seasons for viewing:	Su, F
Map:	USGS Index 7.5'

Getting There

Drive east on US Route 2 from I-5 Everett exit 194. At MP 30, two miles past the town of Gold Bar, turn left (north) onto Reiter Road. Re-start your mileage count. Ignore a left turn onto May Creek Road. At 2.0 miles, and just beyond gravel pits that see a ton of off-road vehicle activity, go left (northwest) on an unpaved power line road. Cross beneath the wires at the 2.3 mile mark.

Right after the transmission lines, leave the better road and go left on a very bad one, still trending northwest. High clearance vehicles are much in order from here on, but the distance is not too great if you must park and walk. At a Y in 3.3 miles, turn right and go slightly up hill. Park in a wide turn-around area after a final tenth of a mile. The road-end situation is due to a bridge washout on May Creek, hostess to Lake Isabel Outlet Falls.

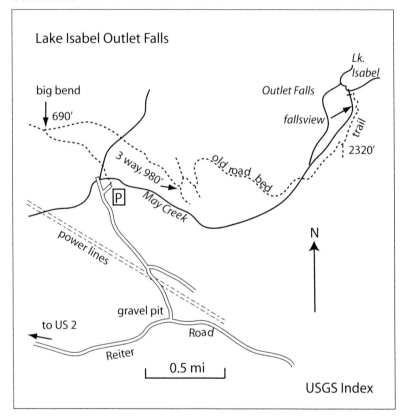

Lake Isabel Outlet Falls

Trail and Falls

The Reiter Road area is off-road heaven to a whole lot of the power crowd, and the lower slopes of these foothill mountains show it. Spun-out gravel, mud-splattered foliage, and ripped-up forest floor are evident everywhere. So too is the noise. Go on a weekend and you will not leave the physical and auditory carnage behind until close to the serenity of lake and falls.

Now afoot, cross May Creek and also an immediate second deep wash. (This one may or may not show running water.) Go right at the next intersection. Due to this area's rampant two and four wheel action the route may not be quite as described here. The operators love carving new branches of their surface warrens. A good checkpoint, however, is found at 0.6 mile. At that point, on obvious old forest road, a switchback swings sharply right (east), and a lesser-used road remnant takes off left (west) from the bend. Go right with the switchback. At 1.4 miles encounter a three-way junction. Go left, but in only a tenth of a mile leave that choice and swing right to climb more steeply. In another quarter mile curve left on a switchback. Here the road steepens once again and becomes very washed out and rocky.

The combination of steep and rough does not let up until about the 2.5-mile mark, where a trail of unknown destination appears on the right side of the road. Shortly, begin to hear May Creek on the right and pass a campsite on the left. At 2.8 miles, and 1900 feet of elevation, cross May Creek on a bridge built of parallel logs. The steep and the rough footing return immediately. Two-tenths of a mile above the creek a tributary stream has badly washed out the way, making the road appear to climb to the right in the creek bed itself. Bear left instead on a crude track, unbelievably forced by wheels. The way snakes through the washed out gully and soon becomes forest road with a good and welcome tread.

At 3.2 miles, not far from the twisted turns through the washout, look carefully for a trail on the left. Where it leaves the old road the path is unsigned, but an 8-inch thick alder by the trail opening carries a blaze. Head up the trail. Sixty feet from its start, the tread turns sharply left. At 3.5 miles and 2,500 feet in elevation, the terrain (finally) flattens out at the base of the waterfall.

Lake Isabel Outlet Falls is tall and lovely, and the lake is a gem in its own right. Getting up to the lakeshore from the base of the waterfall, however, is a hand-over-hiking-boot affair. It is a climb of 340 vertical feet in only 0.2 mile, but worth every claw hold. Bad as this makes it sound, the route is not anything like a rock scramble on open ledges. The way is wooded; there's always something good to hold onto.

Well, since you've come this far . . . .

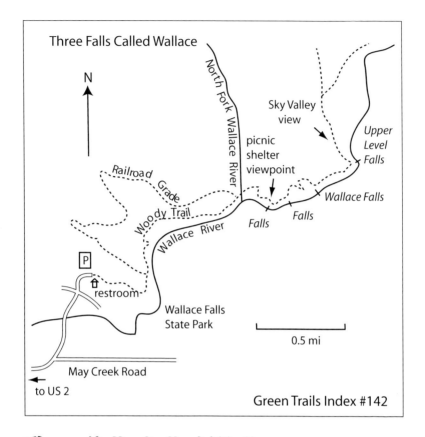

Three Falls Called Wallace

N

North Fork Wallace River

Sky Valley view

Upper Level Falls

picnic shelter viewpoint

Railroad Grade

Woody Trail

Wallace River

Wallace Falls

Falls

Falls

Falls

P

restroom

Wallace Falls State Park

0.5 mi

May Creek Road

to US 2

Green Trails Index #142

Three Falls Called Wallace

The tumultuous Wallace River drops over eight hundred vertical feet in just one half of a river mile. There are four waterfall views in that reach, spaced out along one mile of moderate to strenuous trail. One of them is a look from the top of a plunge, so the lot is counted as three. Taken together they expose more than five hundred vertical feet of that explosive stretch of river. The four views, plus a non-waterfall peek out over the Skykomish Valley, are described in turn.

To get to the falls, leave I-5 at Everett exit 194 and drive east on US 2 to MP 27.9 in Gold Bar. The left turn (north) is signed "Wallace Falls State Park." The 1.7 mile driving route is well signed at several changes of road name and direction.

Rule number one, especially on nice weekend days, is to get to the park early or forget it. Wallace Falls is one of the most popular walking attractions in the state. Its parking area is often completely inadequate. Arrive in late morning and an additional half-mile walk may be necessary to get from roadside parking to the trailhead.

Picnic Shelter Viewpoint

ᗜᗜᗜᗜ

Type of falls:	Plunge
Height of falls:	75 to 100 feet
Approach:	Hike 4.8 miles
Starting elevation:	320 feet
Falls elevation:	870 feet
Difficulty:	Moderate
Seasons for viewing:	Su, Sp, F, W
Map:	USGS Goldbar 7.5'

Getting There
Find the driving directions in Three Falls Called Wallace.

Trail and Falls
The trail starts near the rest rooms in the northeast corner of the under-sized parking loop and follows power-line right-of-way for 0.4 mile. Once in the woods there is a choice of walking routes: An abandoned logging railroad grade continues straight ahead, while the Woody Trail goes off to the right. (Add one mile to the mileages given if you opt for the longer, though gentler ascent of the Railroad Grade.) Esthetic preference says to go right on the Woody Trail. It drops to cross a small stream and then co-zies up to the photogenic Wallace River. It soon climbs moderately away from the stream and, at 1.9 miles from parking, once again merges with the Railroad Grade.

A short distance beyond the intersection of routes the trail crosses the North Fork Wallace River. (The blending of the two forks takes place not far below the bridge.) After a longish half-mile stint a sturdy picnic shelter comes into view, bringing with it the awesome sight of the first of several "Wallace Falls." A stairway leads down to a second view, this one of the dynamic flow disappearing over a watery leap.

Mid-level Viewpoint
◊◊◊◊◊

Type of falls:	Two-Tiered Plunge
Height of falls:	265 feet
Approach:	Hike 5.4 miles
Starting elevation:	320 feet
Falls elevation:	1120 feet
Difficulty:	Strenuous
Seasons for viewing:	Sp, Su, F, W
Map:	USGS Goldbar 7.5'

Getting There
Find the driving directions above in Three Falls Called Wallace.

Trail and Falls
 The trail segments leading from level to level are easy to locate. As stirring as the first gems on this string of jewels may be, the effect is even more spectacular at Mid-Level Viewpoint. (Mid-Level is shown on the accompanying map-graphic as *Wallace Falls* because it is so labeled on the Goldbar 7.5' topo.) Follow the slightly steeper trail upward three-tenths of a mile, 2.7 total miles from the trailhead, to a railed platform. Seen from there, a column of white water hurtles 165 feet to a frothy pool, where it rests only briefly. Seemingly anxious to be on its way, the swirl of aqueous green spills from its pause-point to plunge another hundred feet. This 265-foot blaze of silver can be seen from US Route 2 more than eight air miles away. On your approach drive, in the vicinity of the western edge of the town of Startup, look for a shimmering streak of light low on the flank of Mount Stickney to the northeast.

Sky Valley Viewpoint

This site is unrated because its falls-view is of the top of the Mid-Level drop. The scenic focus here is out over "Sky" Valley. The view platforms are two separate railed overlooks, and are found a strenuous four-tenths of a mile above the Mid-Level Viewpoint. The place is 3.1 miles one-way from parking. At 1,400 feet in elevation, this viewpoint is not always a viable winter walk.

Upper-Level Viewpoint

ᗖᗖᗖᗖᗖ

Type of falls:	Plunge
Height of falls:	200 feet
Approach:	Hike 7.0 miles
Starting elevation:	320 feet
Falls elevation:	1600 feet
Difficulty:	Strenuous
Seasons for viewing:	Sp, Su, F
Map:	USGS Goldbar 7.5'

Getting There
Find the driving directions above under Three Falls Called Wallace.

Trail and Falls
The Upper-Level Viewpoint is four-tenths of a mile above the Sky Valley Viewpoint, and is 3.5 miles from parking. This last waterfall is another exciting one. Its action is arranged in an order which is the reverse of that of Mid-Level falls. Here a fifty-foot drop comes first, followed by a plunge of at least 150 vertical feet. The trail is a rough and root-filled way, but well worth the extra effort. Given its proximity to Mount Stickney, along with its 1,600 feet in elevation, the Upper-Level site may at times have too much snow underfoot for winter hiking.

Trail to Bridal Veil Falls

Bridal Veil Falls (Mount Index)

Type of falls:	Segmented Slide
Height of falls:	85 to 95 feet
Approach:	Hike 4.4 miles
Starting elevation:	560 feet
Falls elevation:	1620 feet
Difficulty:	Moderate
Seasons for viewing:	Sp, Su, F, W
Map:	USGS Index 7.5'

Getting There

From I-5 exit 194 in Everett, drive US 2 to MP 35.2, and turn right (south) on Mount Index Road. In 0.3 mile turn right (south) on Spur Road 109, and almost immediately go left into the large, graveled Serene Lake Trail parking area. There are modern pit toilets at the site.

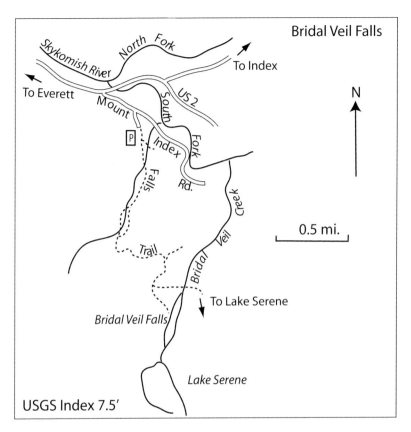

Bridal Veil Falls

N

0.5 mi.

To Lake Serene

Bridal Veil Falls

Lake Serene

USGS Index 7.5'

Trail and Falls

Mount Index, a finger-like tower of rock, and its nearby namesake town are located close to the confluence of the hearty North and South Forks of the Skykomish River. Prior to the time of a rail crossing of Stevens Pass, Index town site was known as *Gunn's Place*. It was a needed trading post and rest stop on a historic walking route to eastern Washington, via the North Fork and Dishpan Gap.

For nearly half of its length the Serene Lake Trail follows a gated and no longer driven forest road. Forks in the road are well signed. In 0.2 mile contend with a road washout by going up along the stream's right (west) bank. There are better crossing sites than the one directly in the washed-out roadway.

At 0.6 mile the old road again becomes badly washed out, but an easy crossing leads to rough but decent trail on the west bank. After only a tenth of a mile of detour, re-cross to the east bank. The road/trail then veers northeast away from the water. In this stretch, look upward for a view of the summit spire of the North Peak of Mount Index.

The road levels at 1.4 miles as another forest road comes in from the left (northeast). Shortly, at 1240 feet in elevation, real trail leaves the old road on a right-leading curve. The change is signed. Good trail drops slightly to negotiate the gully of a small stream before forking at 1.6 miles. The Lake Serene Trail follows the left tine, while a sign points right to Bridal Veil Falls in another 0.6 mile, 2.2 total miles from parking. The last half mile contains many sections of built-in stairs and lots of plank-built causeway.

The pretty waterfall, though nearly a hundred feet high, makes up a small fraction of the hundreds of actual vertical feet of drop along Index Creek. The terrain leading to most of the remaining falling water, however, is far too dangerous for inclusion. The greater "Bridal Veil" can be appreciated from US 2, a mile or more distant. The safe and sane view at trail's end is a many-segmented beauty of considerable power. For all of its volume, this descent is accomplished with more grace than is many another waterfall.

Eagle Falls

Eagle Falls

Type of falls:	Flume/Slide
Height of falls:	25 to 35 feet
Approach:	Drive
Falls elevation:	680 feet
Seasons for viewing:	Sp, Su, F, and W
Map:	USGS Index 7.5'

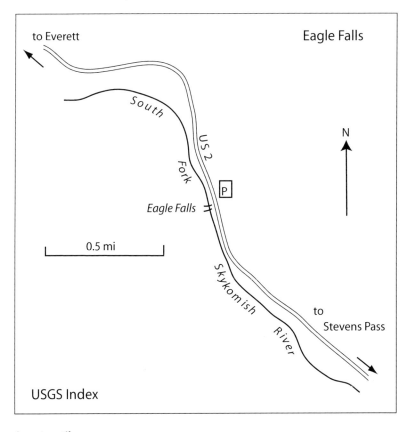

Getting There

Drive US 2 from Everett exit 194 to MP 39. (This assumes that missing milepost number thirty-nine has been replaced. Why not be prudent and measure a mile from MP 38?) Look for a distinctive rocky slot where the highway builders blasted through a narrow rib of bedrock. Park on the right side of the highway in a small paved turnout just before the distinctive band of rock.

The Falls

The rock rib giving construction crews only a bit of resistance was no match either for the Skykomish River. The water, with its load of abrasive sediments, cut through that same band long before the engineers arrived. Over the millennia, by repeated under-cuttings and collapses, it then managed to move the drop-off point of the falls a hundred and fifty-feet upstream.

The two-tiered fall can be seen from the road, though rough scramble trails lead down to better views amid all the spray and other watery ruckus.

Alpine Falls

Type of falls:	Chute
Height of falls:	40 feet
Approach:	Drive
Falls elevation:	1440 feet
Seasons for viewing:	Sp, Su, F
Map:	USGS Scenic 7.5'

Getting There

Drive US 2 east from I-5 Everett exit 194. Park in a large turnout on the right (south) at MP 55.3. It is just before the highway bridge over the Tye River.

The Falls

Along the rear (south) edge of the turnout, find and follow the remnants of an old road a short way through trees to partial views of the top of this segmented waterfall. Good views from the base of the descent can be had with an equally short, though strenuous down climb of a steep slope. A mass of raised bedrock causes the river to divide, making the drop look like two separate waterfalls. The twins reunite smoothly at the bottom.

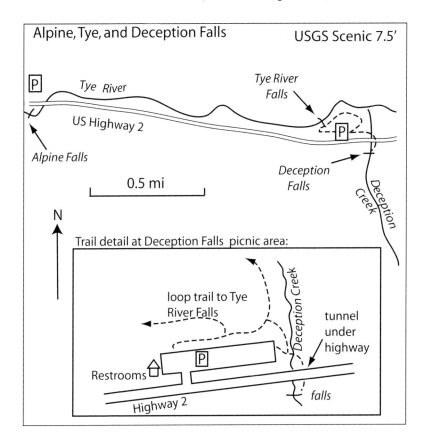

Alpine, Tye, and Deception Falls — USGS Scenic 7.5'

Deception Falls

Type of falls:	Plunge/Tumble
Height of falls:	60 to 100 feet
Approach:	Walk 0.2-mile
Falls elevation:	1920 feet
Seasons for viewing:	Sp, Su, F, W
Map:	USGS Scenic 7.5'

Getting There

Drive US 2 east from I-5 Everett exit 194. Park at the Deception Falls Wayside Area on the left (north) side of the highway at MP 56.6.

The Falls

Locate a stairway at the eastern end of parking. Take it down to a walkway leading quickly to the frenetic creek and its bridged crossing. Stone steps lead upward and then beneath the highway on a steel railinged balcony. On the south side of US 2 there are view platforms close below the falls. The tunnel-like amplification of sounds, as well as the placement of the walkway (only a few feet above the frenzy) heightens the whole experience. The site is a well-planned enhancement of a natural attraction.

Tye River Falls

Type of falls:	Plunge
Height of falls:	12 feet
Approach:	Hike 1.8 miles
Starting elevation:	1800 feet
Falls elevation:	1620 feet
Difficulty:	Moderate
Seasons for viewing:	Sp, Su, F, and W
Map:	USGS Scenic 7.5'

Getting There

Follow driving directions for Deception Falls, the previous entry. The Tye River loop trail and Deception Falls access trail share the same parking area.

Trail and Falls

In winter, two to five feet of snow will likely be covering this trail, but the walk is so popular that the trail remains broken in nearly all the time. For the snowy season, carry a pair of ski poles for balance when walking in the sometimes rutty, frozen footprints.

The start of the loop trail is to the right of the rest rooms at the west end of parking. The paved beginning of the trail continues east as a wheelchair-accessible route of about one-tenth of a mile to the bridge over Deception Creek. For the walk along the Tye River, however, turn left (north) a hundred-fifty feet from the trail start and follow the path leftward again (westerly) as it descends through old growth timber. It crosses an overflow channel of Deception Creek before rising slightly to reach the Tye at 0.4 mile. Downstream of this first vantage point the Tye swirls on into a low walled canyon.

When proceeding upstream on the wide trail, be sure to take side stairways down to more views of the dynamic waterway. The first is for views of Tye River Falls. The river pours through a choke point to drop several feet, only to slam into a rock wall nearly at right angles to its path. The slot looks like it could be a faultline, but it technically is a *joint*, a crack between many of the huge blocks of bedrock found in the area. The Tye's entire flow races away in the deep trench to go around the obstacle. Look closely at the left or downstream side of the wall. At high water the river washes over the obstacle and is slowly carving itself an escape notch. Given time, it will succeed.

The second stairway leads to a small but powerful bonus waterfall. Look upstream from the viewing platform to see Deception Creek entering the Tye River on the right.

At 0.8 mile rejoin the paved way. Go left (east) to pass beneath US 2 to views of Deception Falls. (See Deception Falls, page 127.) Turn right (west) to bypass Deception Falls and return directly to parking in a final tenth of a mile.

North Fork Skykomish River

The north and south forks of the Skykomish come together a little way west of the town of Index. The merger can be seen from the South Fork Bridge on US 2 just east of milepost 35. To reach the waterfalls of the North Fork, leave US 2 at MP 35.6, signed for Index, and go left (north) on the North Fork Skykomish Road. Zero out your mileage count at the turn off US Route 2.

The North Fork Skykomish Road becomes FR 63 soon after passing the beginning of the bridge (left) to Index, just shy of MP 1.

Bear Falls

Type of falls:	Chute/Plunge
Height of falls:	30 to 50 feet
Approach:	Walk 0.2 mile
Starting elevation:	1430 feet
Falls elevation:	1390 feet
Difficulty:	Strenuous
Seasons for viewing:	Sp, Su, F
Map:	USGS Monte Cristo 7.5'

Getting There

Find the area driving directions under North Fork Skykomish River (above). Parking for Bear Falls is found 12.2 miles along the North Fork Road (FR 63) but can be a challenge to locate. With the road curving leftward at that point, a narrow, crushed rock turnout (long enough for two to three cars) slopes away from the road on the right. Apart from these nebulous clues there is nothing else distinctive about the correct place, and there are no signs at all. It greatly helps to note your own odometer reading when you pass the west or *second* entrance to Troublesome Creek Campground at roughly the 11.0 mile mark. After having driven another eight-tenths of a mile or so, proceed slowly and look for the curving road scenario described above.

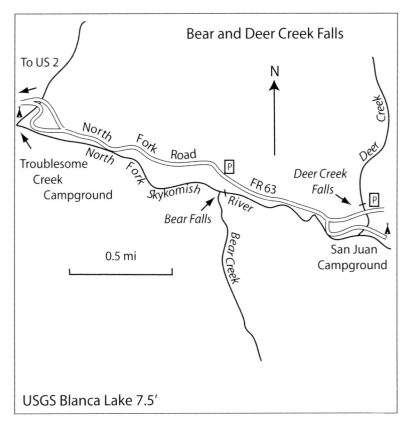

Trail and Falls

Two or more easily found paths lead south out of the turnout. All are worthy of exploration, but the more westerly route goes to the waterfall near where Bear Creek enters on the south bank of the river. Other sites, reachable with some degree of athleticism once in the rugged gorge, are combinations of chutes, plunges, and swirling drops in a maze of deeply cut bedrock. This is a three-droplet waterfall in a five-droplet setting. Be very cautious on the sloping and slick riverside ledges.

Deer Creek Falls

Type of falls:	Plunge/Tumble
Height of falls:	115 to 125 feet
Approach:	Drive
Falls elevation:	1700 feet
Seasons for viewing:	Sp, Su, F
Map:	USGS Blanca Lake 7.5'

Getting There

Find the area driving directions under North Fork Skykomish River. At a fork in FR 63, 13.9 miles from US 2, go left and uphill on a newer section of paved road. (The Y-junction is not shown on the 1965 edition of the USGS Blanca Lake 7.5' topographic map.) In one-tenth of a mile more, where the road levels out between rises, park on either side of where Deer Creek crosses the road beneath a metal grating over a U-shaped concrete culvert. About two-thirds of the waterfall can be seen two hundred-fifty feet upstream. Its twisted route set between deeply eroded walls prevents full exposure.

Views of Deer Creek Falls are enhanced somewhat, but not to three-drop status, by making a rough scramble up the creek bed. It is not a particularly dangerous ascent, but it does offer the possibility of leg or ankle injuries as well as a good dunking.

Rocky Gorge

Rocky Gorge is more steep rapid than waterfall, and is unrated. However the place is categorized, the North Fork Skykomish River goes into diagonal descent mode in the area from 18.5 to 18.8 miles along FR 63. It is worth the stop.

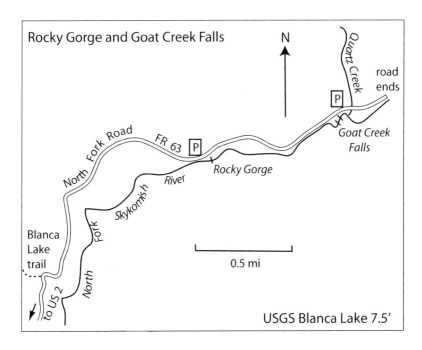

Goat Falls

Type of falls:	Plunge/Slide
Height of falls:	25 to 50 feet
Approach:	Drive or walk 0.1 mile
Falls elevation:	2400 feet
Seasons for viewing:	Sp, Su, F
Map:	USGS Blanca Lake 7.5'

Getting There

Find the area driving directions under North Fork Skykomish River. Follow FR 63 to where pavement ends at a prominent road junction at 16.7 miles. Go left with FR 63 as it turns sharply northeast. After passing the area of Rocky Gorge (18.5 to 18.8 miles) look for a road spur on the right (southeast) side of the road, 20.0 miles from US 2. If you cross the bridge over Quartz Creek you have missed the spot by a bit more than a tenth of a mile. Park in the spur, which quickly leads to a popular campsite, or find ample space on the shoulder of wide FR 63.

The Falls

A short, easy pathway leads from the campsite to the top of the slide portion of Goat Falls. Other waterfall adventurers have forged a steep and rough way to the foot of this fifteen-foot drop. While the view gained is superior to that from the top, it does come with a degree of strenuous labor.

The drive-to portion of Goat Falls is two or three hundred feet back down FR 63. The lower, or second, of two drops is seen from that vantage point as a tri-segmented run of twenty-five to thirty feet. A look upstream yields a face-on view of the upper falls, a funnel-shaped slide past restricting bedrock walls.

A short way beyond the crossing of Quartz Creek FR 63 comes to an end in one of the longest trailhead parking areas in the North Cascades. Three different hiking options lead out of it, all climbing to the Pacific Crest Trail. One, the North Fork Skykomish Trail, is the prehistoric Native American route to Lake Wenatchee and eastern Washington. Mountain men, settlers and mineral prospectors used the trail before it was supplanted by the route over Stevens Pass.

Seattle – Snoqualmie Pass

The three forks of the Snoqualmie system drain most of the northeastern quarter of King County before surrendering it all to the Snohomish River. All waterfalls in the Snoqualmie triumvirate are accessible from I-90, the exit numbers of which correspond closely to distances east of Seattle.

Main Stream and South Fork Snoqualmie Rivers

McCauley Falls

Type of falls:	Veil/Slide/Tumble
Height of falls:	250 feet
Approach:	Drive
Falls elevation:	200 feet
Seasons for viewing:	Sp, F, W
Map:	USGS Monroe 7.5'

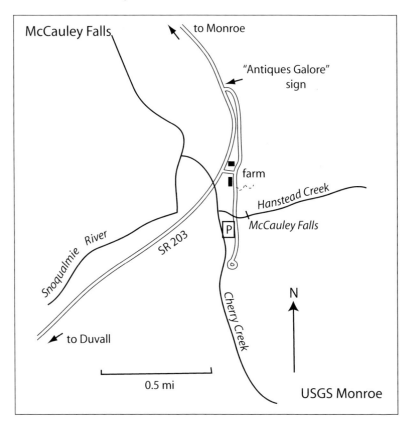

Getting There

Leave I-90 at exit 22. Drive the Preston-Fall City Road 4.5 miles north to a junction with SR 202 in Fall City. Turn right on SR 202 and immediately cross the Snoqualmie River. Once across the bridge, turn left (north) on SR 203. At 17.7 miles from I-90, nearly three miles north of Duval, turn right (sharply southeast) on a dirt road marked only by an "Antiques Galore" sign. The dirt road doubles back south to nearly parallel the main road. Reset your odometer. In 0.6 mile pass very close to the rear of some farm buildings, and cross over a culvert at the base of the falls just shy of a mile. The waterfall is on the left (east) side of the dirt road.

The Falls

The veil/slide portion of McCauley Falls is 50 to 60 feet high with the tumble section dropping all the way to the road. Parking is very limited. The only turn-around is another four-tenths of a mile along the dirt road.

Snoqualmie Falls

Getting There

Type of falls:	Segmented Plunge
Height of falls:	268 feet
Approach:	Drive, Wheelchair accessible
Falls elevation:	390 feet
Seasons for viewing:	Sp, Su, F, W
Map:	USGS Snoqualmie 7.5'

Getting There

Reach Snoqualmie Falls by leaving I-90 at exit 22. Drive north 4.5 miles to Fall City and a junction with State Route 202. Turn right (east), crossing the Snoqualmie River, and continue east on SR 202 to Snoqualmie Falls Park, 8.5 miles from I-90.

Be sure to leave your vehicle in a recognized falls parking area. Parking near the chain-link fenced viewing walkway is legal but limited. In response to growing demand, more spaces at ever-higher levels have been constructed on the hillside across the road. Do not park in spaces reserved for guests of the restaurant, for citations are liberally handed out.

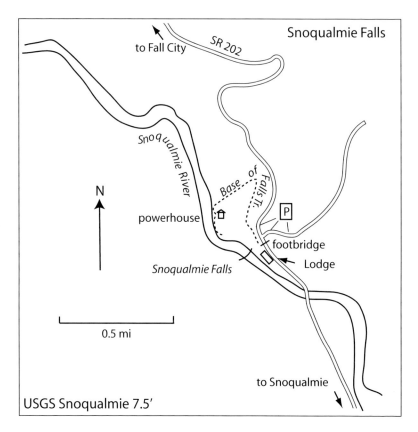

The Falls

This is an extremely popular tourist destination, so plan your visit for other than nice weekends between spring break and Halloween. There is no mystery surrounding where to stand in order to look down on the spectacular drop. Snoqualmie Falls Park and Snoqualmie Falls Lodge occupy the entire south side of the highway at that point. Anywhere there is space at the fence guarding the chasm there will also be good views.

For the hardy, a one-mile round-trip walking route leads to a view platform at river level, though the site is some distance back from the actual base of the falls. The route, which starts between the rest-room facility and the view fence, is moderately steep but with good footing.

Trail along South Fork Snoqualmie River to Twin Falls

Twin Falls – South Fork Snoqualmie River

Type of falls:	Slide/Veil
Height of falls:	100 to 120 feet
Approach:	Hike 2.8 miles
Starting elevation:	600 feet
Falls elevation:	940 feet
Difficulty:	Moderate
Seasons for viewing:	Sp, Su, F, and W
Map:	USGS Chester Morse Lake 7.5'

Getting There

Leave I-90 at exit 34. Turn right (south) onto 468th Ave. SE for 0.6 mile. A left turn there, (east) on 159th Street, leads to road's end and Twin Falls Park when 1.8 total miles from I-90.

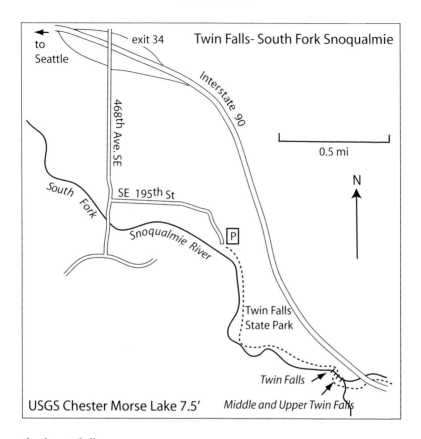

to Seattle

exit 34

Twin Falls- South Fork Snoqualmie

Interstate 90

468th Ave. SE

South Fork

SE 195th St

Snoqualmie River

P

0.5 mi

N

Twin Falls State Park

Twin Falls

USGS Chester Morse Lake 7.5'   Middle and Upper Twin Falls

Trail and Falls

The title of this entry, *Twin Falls – South Fork Snoqualmie River*, is intended to differentiate it from another twin in the Stillaguamish valley, that of Twin Falls – Ashland Lakes. The falls on the South Fork, actually triplets, are known by some as Upper Snoqualmie Falls. They are reached by walking a well-maintained trail along the picturesque river before climbing considerably upward through old growth forest. A distant view of Twin Falls and a second drop upstream of it is had from a platform at the 0.9 mile mark. Note a splendid seven-foot-diameter Douglas fir tree a tenth of a mile beyond the view site.

At 1.4 miles reach an obvious and well-constructed stairway leading down to viewing platforms for this artfully endowed waterfall. Its top thirty-feet ripple steeply to splay into shimmering ribbons for a captivating descent to the waiting river.

Middle Twin Falls

Type of falls:	Slide/Plunge
Height of falls:	25 feet
Approach:	Hike 3.0 miles
Starting elevation:	600 feet
Falls elevation:	1100 feet
Difficulty:	Moderate
Seasons for viewing:	Sp, Su, F, and W
Map:	USGS Chester Morse Lake 7.5′

Getting There

Follow the driving directions to Twin Falls, above.

Trail and Falls

Middle Twin Falls is only a tenth of a mile upstream from Twin Falls on the same trail. A park sign confusingly calls this drop "Lower" Twin Falls, yet it lies upstream between Twin and Upper Twin Falls. To reach the very best view of Middle Falls, continue 0.1 mile upstream from the top of Twin Falls' wooden stairway to a sturdy bridge over the river. Middle Falls is upstream of that crossing. Look downstream for a top view of Twin Falls.

Upper Twin Falls

Type of falls:	Tumble/Plunge
Height of falls:	60 feet
Approach:	Hike 3.2 miles
Starting elevation:	600 feet
Falls elevation:	1160 feet
Difficulty:	Moderate
Seasons for viewing:	Sp, Su, F, and W
Map:	USGS Chester Morse Lake 7.5′

Getting There

Follow the driving and trailhead directions for Twin Falls.

Trail and Falls

A viewing area for Upper Twin Falls is found 0.1 mile upstream from the bridge below Middle Twin Falls. The river tumbles through a rock-walled mini-canyon before resuming its horizontal rush to Middle Twin Falls.

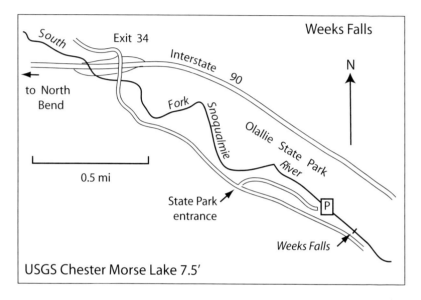

USGS Chester Morse Lake 7.5'

Weeks Falls

Type of falls:	Segmented/Tumble
Height of falls:	50 feet
Falls elevation:	1240 feet
Approach:	Walk 0.1 mile
Difficulty:	Easy
Seasons for viewing:	Sp, Su, F, and W
Map:	USGS Chester Morse Lake 7.5'

Getting There

Leave I-90 at exit 38 and turn right (south) for 0.7 mile. Take the left choice at a fork in the road and drive into Ollalie State Park. Go past the park manager's residence to the end of the road and park on the shoulders of a turnaround loop, 1.1 miles from I-90.

There is no eastbound freeway entrance to I-90 at Ollalie State Park. In order to go east upon leaving the park it is necessary to go *west* to exit 34 and use it as a U-turn route.

The Falls

Though this waterfall is in the South Fork Snoqualmie River, it easily fits into a day of seeing Snoqualmie Falls as well as the three falls in Twin Falls State Park. The waterfall is in view from parking, but a wheelchair-accessible walkway leads much closer to it.

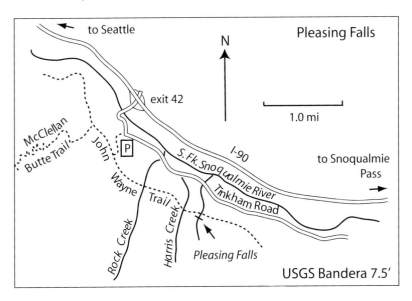

Pleasing Falls

Type of falls:	Tumble/Slide
Height of falls:	40 feet
Approach:	Hike 4.2 miles
Starting elevation:	1500 feet
Falls elevation:	1940 feet
Difficulty:	Moderate
Seasons for viewing:	Sp, F, W
Map:	USGS Bandera 7.5', or Green Trails Bandera #206

Getting There

Drive I-90 to exit 42 signed for Tinkham Road, FR 55. Go south and cross the South Fork Snoqualmie River. In a bit over 0.3 mile, turn right on FR 5500 - 101, and proceed to parking for the McClellan Butte Trail, 0.6 mile from I-90.

Trail and Falls

Pass beneath power lines 0.2 mile up the McClellan Butte Trail. At 0.4 mile ignore an obvious abandoned railroad bed. Continue upward to the 0.5 mile point where the trail intersects a very drivable roadway. This is the abandoned right-of-way of the historic Milwaukee Railroad, now the John Wayne Trail located within Iron Horse State Park. A right turn (west) leads to the continuation of the McClellan Butte Trail (highly recommended for great views); but for Pleasing Falls go left (east) on John Wayne Trail.

The wide and level way passes over Rock Creek at 1.3 miles and over Harris Creek at 1.9 miles, both signed. Pleasing Falls appears suddenly on the right at 2.1 miles from parking. Its small creek drops over human-made cliffs directly on the south side of the road/trail. The place is just east of AT&T buried cable marker #745.

Humpback Creek Falls

Type of falls:	Tumble
Height of falls:	60 feet
Approach:	Hike 0.5 mile
Starting elevation:	1920 feet
Falls elevation:	2120 feet
Difficulty:	Moderate
Seasons for viewing:	Sp, Su. F
Map:	USGS Snoqualmie Pass 7.5′

Getting There

Drive I-90 to exit 47, signed for Denny Creek, Asahel Curtis Picnic Area, and Lake Annette Trail. Turn south to quickly join the Tinkham Road. Turn left (east) to road's end and parking for Lake Annette. The loop turn-around is 0.6 mile from I-90. Do walk the trail to the left of the signboard, for it is the Asahel Curtis Nature Trail, oldest such designated in the state.

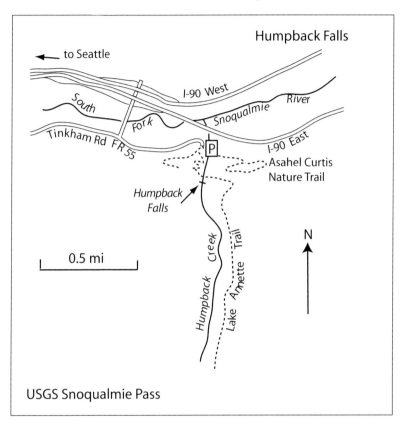

Trail and Falls

There are trails to both right and left of an information signboard at the east end of the parking area.

For Humpback Falls, start out on FR 5590 to the right of the signboard, but soon go left on Trail #1019 toward Lake Annette. The waterfall is found a quarter mile along the way and just upstream of a photo-op wooden bridge over Humpback Creek.

Keekwulee Falls

Keekwulee Falls

Type of falls:	Slide/Plunge
Height of falls:	105 to 125 feet
Approach:	Hike 4.0 miles
Starting elevation:	2320 feet
Falls elevation:	3120 feet
Difficulty:	Strenuous
Seasons for viewing:	Sp, Su, F
Map:	USGS Snoqualmie Pass 7.5'

Getting There

Drive I-90 to exit 47. Restart your mileage count. Go north over the freeway and turn right (east) on Denny Creek Road, FR 58. Follow the Denny Creek signs 2.6 miles to the campground, where the road splits. Go right. From there things happen fast: at 2.8 miles turn left onto FR 5830. In another tenth of a mile pass trailhead parking for Franklin Falls #1036, cross a bridge over the South Fork Snoqualmie River, and then, 3.1 miles from I-90, arrive at road's end and parking for Denny Creek Trail #1014.

Trail and Falls

The trail rises at only a moderate rate, but it earns a "strenuous" rating for its roughness. There are lots of rocks and roots to dodge.

Cross Denny Creek at a strong 0.4 mile and, after passing beneath the westbound lanes of I-90, cross the creek again, 1.3 miles and 2,800 feet in elevation, getting closer to the goal of Keekwulee Falls. This upper creek crossing used to be via a foot-log, but no longer. The wide creek must now be rock-hopped or waded, which can be a problem in times of high run-off. Once across, do not follow the old trail downstream. Look right. The lesser used way is easy to find.

View this impressive falls while standing in Denny Creek Trail. A good spot is where the path skirts a boulder field 2.0 miles from parking. Not long ago a young man was killed in a slip and tumble from the top of the falls. Why oh why go up there? Certainly not for the view.

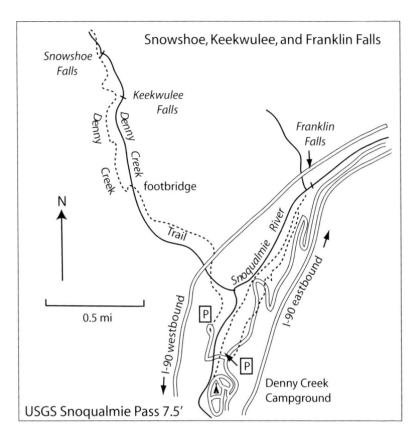

Snowshoe, Keekwulee, and Franklin Falls

Snowshoe Falls

Keekwulee Falls

Denny

Denny Creek

Creek

Franklin Falls

footbridge

N

Trail

Snoqualmie River

0.5 mi

I-90 westbound

I-90 eastbound

P

P

Denny Creek
Campground

USGS Snoqualmie Pass 7.5'

Snowshoe Falls

This one-hundred-foot or taller waterfall is unrated because it is about 60% hidden by tree trunks, branches, and brush. Any attempt to improve on the situation becomes very dangerous indeed. Follow the trail to Keekwulee Falls (presented above) then climb semi-steep switchbacks for another half-mile. After the last zigzag the way levels out at 3,640 feet in elevation. It then parallels the creek for a final tenth of a mile. The fall will announce itself.

Franklin Falls

Type of falls:	Plunge
Height of falls:	85 to 100 feet
Approach:	Hike 2.0 miles
Starting elevation:	2200 feet
Falls elevation:	2580
Difficulty:	Moderate
Seasons for viewing:	Sp, Su, F
Map:	USGS Snoqualmie Pass 7.5'

Getting There

Follow the driving directions for Keekwulee Falls. The trailhead for Franklin Falls Trail #1036 is 0.2 mile before Denny Creek Trail #1014, and on the same road.

Trail and Falls

Franklin Falls Trail #1036 follows the right bank of the South Fork Snoqualmie River upstream. Thousands of tree roots crisscross the trail, so watch your footwork to avoid injury. Four-tenths of a mile from parking the river sports an unheralded and picturesque fifteen-foot waterfall. Upstream from this small falls to Franklin Falls the dynamic waterway is all gorge. At Franklin, the entire river is forced to leap from a cliff to a wide pool below.

There is a shorter walk to Franklin Falls. At the point where driving directions say to turn left on FR 5830, go straight east instead. In one mile, where the road turns sharply away from the river, look for a sign announcing the route of the Historic Snoqualmie Pass Wagon Road. Park there in a turnout. Walk the trail behind the sign for about eighty-feet and turn right at a junction. The route intersects Franklin Falls Trail #1036 in another few hundred feet. Go right at that point, upstream, and reach the falls in another tenth of a mile, only two-tenths total miles from the road. Of course, "shorter" means skipping the sights and sounds of the crashing river gorge.

Marten Creek Falls

Taylor River

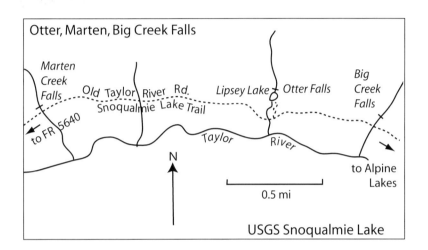

Otter, Marten, Big Creek Falls

Marten Creek Falls

Type of falls:	Flume
Height of falls:	50 to 100 feet
Approach:	Hike 5.6 miles
Starting elevation:	1180 feet
Falls elevation:	1880 feet
Difficulty:	Moderate
Seasons for viewing:	Sp, Su, F, W
Maps:	USGS Lake Philippa 7.5' and
	USGS Snoqualmie Lake 7.5'

Getting There

Drive I-90 to North Bend exit 34. Reset your mileage and go north on 468th Avenue SE for 0.7 mile. Turn right (north) on SE Middle Fork Road.

Take either direction when the route forks for Lake Dorothy Road. The forks reunite in a mile or two. Pavement on the Middle Fork Road ends at 3.0 miles.

At 8.5 miles the road becomes FR 56 as the Mount Baker Snoqualmie National Forest boundary is crossed. There are rest rooms on the right 11.8 miles from I-90 at the Middle Fork Snoqualmie Trailhead, a major entry point for the Alpine Lakes Wilderness. Cross the Taylor River at 12.2 miles, and then stay straight ahead (north) on FR 5640 as FR 56 goes sharply right (east). Park at a gated second bridge over the Taylor River. It is closed to vehicle traffic for safety reasons, 12.7 miles from the interstate.

Note: At the time of this writing there were rumblings from the National Forest Service regarding closing the entire hiking route of abandoned Taylor River Road. Check before going.

Trail and Falls
Walk across the bridge. Turn right at a road junction at 0.5 mile, still on the old Taylor River Road. The gradient is gentle, but lots of smooth, slick rocks in the decaying roadbed make for intense footwork scrutiny. At 2.8 miles reach the once stout wood-framed bridge over Marten Creek. Though still sturdy, it is full of ankle-twisting holes. The very enjoyable waterfall is just upstream. For easiest access, follow one of the many boot-driven pathways on Marten Creek's left bank.

Otter Falls

Type of falls:	Flume/Slide
Height of falls:	230 to 260 feet
Approach:	Hike 8.3 miles
Starting elevation:	1180 feet
Falls elevation:	1860 feet
Difficulty:	Moderate
Seasons for viewing:	Sp, F, W
Maps:	USGS Lake Philippa 7.5' and USGS Snoqualmie Lake 7.5'

Otter Falls

Getting There

Follow the driving directions to Marten Creek Falls. The trailhead is the same.

Trail and Falls

Otter Falls is 1.3 miles east of Marten Creek Falls on the abandoned Taylor River Road. Continue east from Marten Creek on the gently rising and descending road-slash-trail until 4.0 miles from parking.

The unmarked side trail to Otter Falls is on the left (north) at that point, but there is a "can't miss" way to locate it. After passing Marten Creek there are no more actual bridges on the way to Otter Falls. Several stream crossings sport culverts of some two feet in diameter, but the outlet creek for Otter Falls boasts a pipe about five feet across its center. Lots of the large rusting culvert is exposed on the downstream side of the route. The waterway has partially washed out both roadbed and culvert.

Right after that distinctive crossing find the first clearing in more than a mile, certainly since the holey plank bridge over Marten Creek. A fading campsite fire-ring, pretty much in the trail itself, is equally indicative of being in the correct place. Two hundred feet east of the clearing look for an unsigned spur trail on the left (north) side of the trail. The path offers a moderate 0.3 mile round-trip to gorgeous Lake Lipsy and its very beautiful Otter Falls.

Early Spring trail conditions

Hike to Otter Falls in any wet season. It was at such a time that the tapestry of its flow moved the author to write *Water on a Wall*, a poem found on the book's dedication page.

Big Creek Falls

Type of falls:	Plunge/Tumble
Height of falls:	120 feet
Approach:	Hike 9.0 miles
Starting elevation:	1180 feet
Falls elevation:	1760 feet
Difficulty:	Moderate
Seasons for viewing:	Sp, Su, F
Map:	USGS Snoqualmie Lake 7.5′

Getting There

Follow the driving directions for Marten Creek Falls. The trailhead is the same.

Trail and Falls

Also read the trail description for Taylor River Road under Marten Creek Falls. Continue eastward from Marten Creek past Otter Falls spur trail at 4.0 total miles. Go another easy half mile, 4.5 miles total, to Taylor River Road's transit of Big Creek. The crossing is on a great looking, ridiculously out of place concrete and steel bridge. Roiling Big Creek Falls is just upstream, and is best viewed from the bridge.

Middle Fork Snoqualmie River

This unspoiled stream comes off the Cascade Crest north of Snoqualmie Pass and about half-way between the pass and the Alpine Lakes Wilderness Area. Running westerly, it comes up against the Mount Si peaks in North Bend. At that point it is forced to the southwest where it joins the mainstream Snoqualmie River.

Kamikaze Falls

Type of falls:	Slide/Plunge/Tumble
Height of falls:	170 to 200 Feet
Approach:	Hike 4.4 miles
Starting elevation:	940 feet
Falls elevation:	2100 feet
Difficulty:	Strenuous
Seasons for viewing:	Sp, F, W
Maps:	USGS Chester Morse Lake 7.5' and USGS Mount Si 7.5'

Getting There

Drive I-90 to exit 32. Go north on 436th Avenue SE for 0.5 mile. Turn left (west) on SE North Bend Way to the 0.8 mile point, and then turn right (north) on SE Mt. Si Road. Pass the Mt. Si trailhead on the left at 3.2 miles.

4.2 miles from I-90, with 480th Avenue SE on the right, turn sharply left into the unsigned Mount Teneriffe trailhead parking area.

Parking space here frequently does not match demand. Neither does it help that the irregular shape of the lot spawns confusion regarding a logical parking order. Try leaving your vehicle in a spot that minimizes the chances of its being pinned in when you come off the trail.

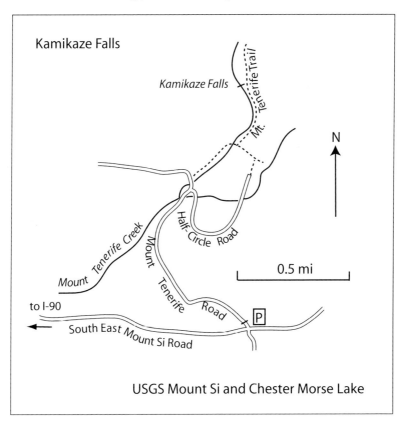

USGS Mount Si and Chester Morse Lake

Trail and Falls

Walk around the gate at the start of Mt. Teneriffe Road and continue for 1.0 mile to a definite three-way intersection of gravel roads. A tiny stream (or streambed) passes beneath Mt. Teneriffe Road just before the junction. (Should you choose, this junction could be the end point of a loop to and from the falls.) Leave Mt. Teneriffe Road and go right (southeast) and uphill on unsigned Half-Circle Road. Half-Circle will gradually do what its name implies, i.e., curve from south to east and then to full north before it tees into Hillside Road, also unsigned, at 1.6 total miles. (The T is more of a sudden left turn to the west, for Hillside's eastward extension appears unused and is heavily brushed over.)

The road becomes more trail-like well before the Hillside/Half Circle connection. At 2.0 miles, Hillside Road ends at the edge of a young hardwood forest. A short path leads west out of clear-cut land to a trail heading north beside Kamikaze Creek. Just into the woods, look on the left (west) for the creek-side extension of the trail going back down to Mt. Teneriffe Road. On the way down, this is the beginning of the loop possibility.

Get ready for some serious elevation gain. The only possible route confusion occurs just below a giant boulder, likely a *glacial erratic*. Such leftovers were dropped wherever the melting ice released them. The steep going is short-lived, however, for the base of wild Kamikaze Falls is reached in only four more tenths of a mile, 2.4 total miles from parking. Finding a better look than what's available from the base of the drop proved to be both difficult and dangerous, but there are more views from higher on the trail.

Going down, watch for that continuation of the creek-side trail mentioned above. Instead of going back out onto Hillside Road, take a right turn (west) to continue down along the attractive creek, intersecting Mt. Teneriffe Road three-tenths of a mile from the route change. Turn left (east) on the gravel road and be back to the intersection with Half-Circle Road in another three-tenths. Retrace your in-coming steps on Mt. Teneriffe Road and be back to parking in an easy mile, 4.4 total miles for the day.

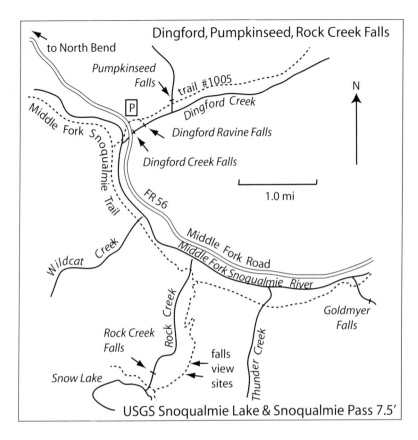

Dingford Creek Falls

Type of falls:	Slide/Plunge
Height of falls:	50 to 80 feet
Approach:	Drive
Falls elevation:	1440 feet
Seasons for viewing:	Sp, Su, F
Map:	USGS Snoqualmie Lake 7.5'

Getting There

Drive I-90 to North Bend exit 34 and go north on 468th Avenue SE for 0.7 mile. Turn right (north) on SE Middle Fork Road. Go either way when the route forks for Lake Dorothy. The choices come back together in a mile or two. Pavement ends at 3.0 miles.

At 8.5 miles the road becomes FR 56 as the Mount Baker Snoqualmie National Forest boundary is crossed. Rest rooms are found on the right, 11.8 miles from I-90, at the Middle Fork Snoqualmie trailhead, a major entry point for the Alpine Lakes Wilderness. Cross a bridge over Taylor River at 12.2 miles. Watch that you stay on FR 56 as it makes a sweeping turn to the right (east). Taylor River Road (FR 5640) continues straight north off the turn.) Restart your mileage count at the intersection.

"Sweeping" also applies to comments concerning the rest of the Middle Fork Road. The route as far as Dingford Creek Falls doesn't exactly demand four-wheel drive, but that's the kindest thing to be said for it. Its surface is paved with grapefruit-to-soccer ball sized rocks, while the roadway itself is a series of giant potholes. Though the resulting bathtubs are often filled with water many inches deep, their bottoms are solid. Wheel-gripping mud is not likely. Six-ply tires or better will add a margin of safety. Take only high-clearance vehicles for the trip, and plan one full hour of driving time – each way – for the 5.8 mile distance from the above intersection. When was the last time you voluntarily drove anywhere at six miles per hour?

The large parking area for Dingford Creek Trail is gratefully reached at 5.6 miles. It feels good to stop there and walk the 0.4 mile round-trip (east) to the bridge over Dingford Creek. The waterfall is nicely viewable from the bridge.

Dingford Ravine

Type of falls:	Plunge/Tumble
Height of falls:	60 to 80 feet
Approach:	Hike 0.7 mile
Starting elevation:	1400 feet
Falls elevation:	1660 feet
Difficulty:	Moderate
Seasons for viewing:	Sp, Su, F
Map:	USGS Snoqualmie Lake 7.5'

Getting There

Follow the driving and parking directions for Dingford Creek Falls.

Trail and Falls

Dingford Creek Trail #1005 starts on the north side of FR 56 across from parking. It climbs steadily before making a definite turn to the left at 0.3 mile. Find an unsigned, though plainly visible pathway leading off the turn leading down toward the audible creek. (Tree branches piled across the un-maintained spur, likely to distinguish it from Trail #1005, may still be evident.) It is perhaps a tenth of a mile round trip to the ravine and back up to Dingford Creek Trail.

Lots of huggable trees provide safe viewing positions along the upper portion of the rugged gorge, but not so downstream. Take care; it only takes one miscalculation. Below, the water enjoys a moment of calm after a gliding descent from a ten-footer, then swirls among boulders before dropping noisily through a vertical slot in glistening bedrock. It foams and crashes until out of sight in the danger zone below.

Pumpkinseed Falls

Type of falls:	Flume
Height of falls:	30 feet
Approach:	Hike 3.0 miles
Starting elevation:	1400 feet
Falls elevation:	2400 feet
Difficulty:	Strenuous
Seasons for viewing:	Sp, F
Map:	USGS Snoqualmie Lake 7.5'

Getting There

Follow the driving directions to Dingford Creek Falls. Parking is the same.

Trail and Falls

The Dingford Creek Trail #1005 begins on the north side of FR 56, across from the graveled parking area. Pass the spur trail to Dingford Ravine and falls at 0.3 mile, and climb somewhat steeply from that point. At 2200 feet cross an aging split-plank bridge over a tiny stream. Soon afterward, enter the Alpine Lakes Wilderness Area and *immediately* notice the stately old growth forest. (Have hope that it really will be saved from the saw.)

The trail's ascent eases off to a gentle upward glide until it curves left-ward into the gully of Pumpkinseed Creek at 1.5 miles, 2400 feet in elevation. The modest waterfall is adjacent to the trail. Paint the scene any way you wish, but on the author's canvas it's going to look like the bald and rounded back sides of a retreating elephant.

Rock Creek Falls

Type of falls:	Plunge/Tumble
Height of falls:	120 to 140 feet
Approach:	Hike 9.4 miles
Starting elevation:	1400 feet
Falls elevation:	2650 feet
Difficulty:	Strenuous
Seasons for viewing:	Sp, Su, F
Map:	USGS Snoqualmie Lake 7.5' and
	USGS Snoqualmie Pass 7.5'

Getting There

Follow the driving directions for Dingford Creek Falls. Parking is the same.

Trail and Falls

The Dingford Creek Trail goes north across from the large graveled parking area, but for Rock Creek Falls, out of the same parking area, go south instead on a connector trail signed for the Middle Fork Snoqualmie Trail. The connector crosses the river via a solid stock bridge in 0.3 mile. Go left (east) on the south bank, upstream, now on the Middle Fork Trail proper. Some checkpoints on the way are provided by significant stream crossings. The first, that of Wildcat Creek is at 1.7 miles. The trail then climbs somewhat steeply to join and follow an old railroad grade a mile to the east. It leaves the gently rising route at 2.7 miles to drop to a foot-log crossing of wide and disheveled Rock Creek, where it climbs once more along the stream's east bank to rejoin the former rail route.

Go right (south) at a trail junction at 2.9 miles, and climb steadily toward Snow Lake and Snoqualmie Pass. After many long switchbacks and a few shorter ones as well, the trail leaves the deep forest for partial heather meadows high on the east bank of Rock Creek. At about twenty-six hundred feet in elevation look across the cirque-like creek basin to see the waterfall, an outlet for Snow Lake, as it bucks and plunges down a steep, largely vegetated headwall.

Lower Cripple Creek Falls

Type of falls:	Tumble
Height of falls:	60 feet
Starting elevation:	1400 feet
Falls elevation:	1280 feet
Difficulty:	Moderate
Seasons for viewing:	Sp, Su, F, W
Map:	USGS Snoqualmie Lake 7.5'

Getting There

Follow the driving directions for Dingford Creek Falls. The trail begins out of the same parking area.

Trail and Falls

Locate the signed Middle Fork Trail Connector on the south edge of the Dingford Creek/Middle Fork Snoqualmie Trail parking area. In 0.3 mile the connector crosses the Middle Fork via an arched and wood-planked stock bridge. When it tees into the Middle Fork Trail, turn right (west) and head down river.

At 1.4 miles from parking, the way crosses Cripple Creek on a good footbridge. Lower Cripple Creek Falls, a welcome interlude in a quiet river valley, speaks out from immediately upstream.

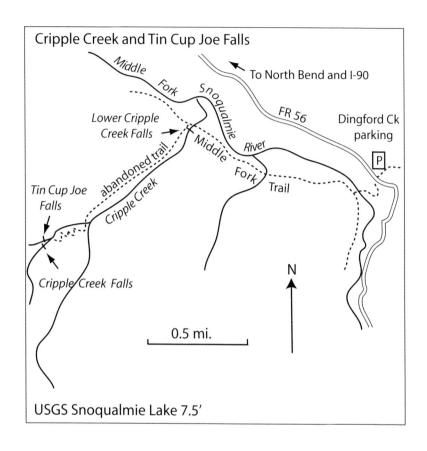

Cripple Creek and Tin Cup Joe Falls

To North Bend and I-90

FR 56

Dingford Ck parking

Middle Fork Snoqualmie River

Lower Cripple Creek Falls

abandoned trail

Cripple Creek

Middle Fork Trail

Tin Cup Joe Falls

Cripple Creek Falls

N

0.5 mi.

USGS Snoqualmie Lake 7.5'

Cripple Creek Falls

Type of falls:	Slide
Height of falls:	100 to 110 feet
Approach:	Hike 5.6 miles
Starting elevation:	1400 feet
Falls elevation:	2300 feet
Difficulty:	Strenuous
Seasons for viewing:	Sp, F
Map:	USGS Snoqualmie Lake 7.5'

Getting There

Follow the driving directions for Dingford Creek Falls. The trail is out of the same parking area.

Trail and Falls

Follow the trail directions for Lower Cripple Creek Falls. About thirty feet west of the west end of the footbridge over Cripple Creek (elevation 1220 feet) look for boot-formed pathways leading up the west bank of Cripple Creek. The going under foot is a bit rough for the next two to four hundred vertical feet, but it works. Another approach is to search for the old trail, for it is still etched into the forest floor. Wandering westward away from the creek and onto higher ground you just might find the track. What works for certain, however, is to stay within a couple hundred feet of Cripple Creek. The creek valley narrows at about sixteen hundred feet in elevation. At that point cliffs and a steep ridge will be seen off to the west. Somewhere in that vicinity identifiable portions of the long abandoned Cripple Creek Trail are sure to be found. With some arduous going, the old route is discernible all the way up to side-by-side Cripple Creek and Tin Cup Joe waterfalls.

At about seventeen hundred feet in elevation, note an impressive stand of Alaska yellow cedars. Their light gray, vertically channeled bark easily distinguishes them from the red-brown skins of the more common western red cedar.

The faint trail leads to a crossing of Cripple Creek at 1800 feet. The lower descents of the two sought-after waterfalls are visible upstream. Across the creek, a small tributary tumbles and splashes down a hundred and fifty-feet of bedrock. Find a crossing of the main creek near this confluence. The way steepens considerably once on the east bank of Cripple Creek but is the safest way to the falls. Once across, look for boot-driven trails upstream through big trees. Getting close.

Stepping stones in Cripple Creek Fall's shallow pause-pool provide great places from which to enjoy the action. Water creates many banners along a broad front as it pours down an impressive wall of rock.

Tin Cup Joe Falls
ᗢᗢᗢᗢ

Type of falls:	Flume
Height of falls:	85 to 100 feet
Approach:	Hike 5.6 miles
Starting elevation:	1400 feet
Falls elevation:	2300 feet
Difficulty:	Strenuous
Seasons for viewing:	Sp, Su, F
Map:	USGS Snoqualmie Lake 7.5′

Getting There

Follow the driving directions for Dingford Creek Falls. The trail leads out of the same parking area.

Trail and Falls

Follow the walking directions for Cripple Creek Falls. Tin Cup Joe Falls is visible from there. Cross the braided channels of Cripple Creek below that waterfall's plunge pool, and then scramble up and over a rough divider of rock, earth, and trees to get to Tin Cup Joe. Both drops regroup momentarily before rushing to bounce down another seventy-five to one hundred feet of the same escarpment. Each of these beauties gets another droplet on the rating scale as soon as the route to them is fed more than a crust of volunteer maintenance.

The Falls of Burnboot Creek

Burnboot Creek (often found on maps spelled 'Burntboot') runs from the Cascade crest to the Middle Fork Snoqualmie River, but a whole lot more than the name of the place is out of the ordinary. In terms of land ownership, difficulty of access, and certainly unspoiled beauty, Burnboot is a very special area.

Both of the named Burnboot Creek waterfalls are found far up the Middle Fork valley on land owned by Northwest Wilderness Programs, a nonprofit corporation. The place is identified on maps as Goldmyer Hot Springs. (That's correct: it is *myer*, not *meyer*.) Because the site is not easy to reach, and because two of the three routes to it are subject to dangerous flow levels of streams which must be forded, the Northwest Wilderness people prefer to advise you of the safest route in at the time of your visit.

Please note that reservations are necessary, an access fee is required, and all visitors are requested to check in at the caretaker cabin upon arrival. The caretaker will gladly give specific directions to the two waterfalls as well as information on bathing in picture-perfect Goldmyer Hot Springs.

Call the Northwest Wilderness Programs office in Seattle at (206) 789-5631. They choose to regulate the number of visitors in order to minimize environmental impact. Please stay on designated trails while on the property. (The mail address is Goldmyer Hot Springs, Northwest Wilderness Programs, 202 N. 85th Street, #106, Seattle, WA, 98103, and their web-site is www.goldmyer.org.)

Getting To Goldmyer Hot Springs

Though three USGS topographic maps are listed for the two Burnboot Creek falls, they do not show the trail and footbridge as currently located. Green Trails Skykomish #175 and Snoqualmie Pass #207 do a better job of it.

To reach Goldmyer Hot Springs by the safest route, drive I-90 to North Bend exit 34, and go north on 468th Avenue SE for 0.7 mile. Turn right (north) on the SE Middle Fork Road. Go either way when the route forks for Lake Dorothy Road. (The roads rejoin in a mile or two). Pavement on the Middle Fork Road ends at 3.0 miles.

The Middle Fork Road becomes FR 56 when 8.5 miles into the drive. There are restrooms on the right 11.8 miles from I-90 at the Middle Fork Snoqualmie Trailhead, a major entry point for Alpine Lakes Wilderness. Cross the Taylor River at 12.2 miles, and then, as FR 5640 (Taylor River Road) goes straight ahead, be sure to stay on FR 56 as it swings sharply right (east). *Restart the mileage count at the turn.*

Though FR 56 is a little rough before getting to the Taylor River Road intersection, it becomes unrelentingly so from that point on. Do not attempt the trip in a low clearance vehicle. Four wheel drive capability is not necessary, but pickups, SUVs, and the like have definite advantages. The first mean place is on a short hill about three miles from where FR 5640 goes off on its own. The grade on FR 56 at that point is all scoops and mounds from people powering up and down it in the loose gravel. The place is between forest service mileposts #15 and #16.

How bad is the Middle Fork Road? Driving out of there one day the author suffered a mild but amusing humiliation. He and his pickup truck were passed by a grinning guy on a mountain bike. Didn't see him again either.

Several roads branch off FR 56 along the route, but all go to the river for one reason or another. FR 56 is never in doubt. The one place that could be called a fork is at 10.2 miles. At that point FR 56 turns more northeasterly and begins to climb. Stay left or straight ahead at all such choice points.

Stop and carefully scout out an especially mean place, an up-hill, ledge-hump in the road at about the 13 mile mark. The road ends at the Dutch Miller Gap trailhead, 14.4 miles from the junction of FR 56 and FR 5640. But . . . .

A quarter mile before road's end there are a few small parking turn-outs near the trail leading down to a footbridge across the Middle Fork Snoqualmie River. Unless there are parked vehicles there the place is difficult to spot on the way in. It is easier to go to the turnaround and drive back the quarter of a mile. It is a 6.0 mile round trip hike to Goldmyer Hot Springs from the trailhead.

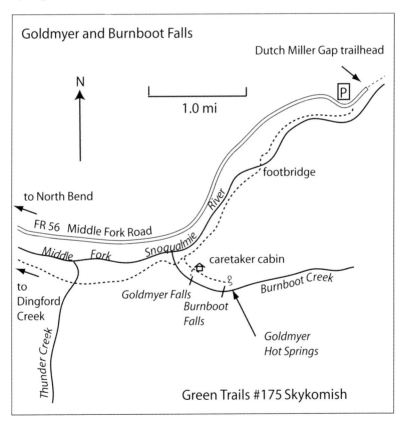

Goldmyer Falls

Type of falls:	Slide/Plunge
Height of falls:	80 to 90 feet
Approach:	Hike 7.0 miles
Starting elevation:	2800 feet
Falls elevation:	1885 feet
Difficulty:	Strenuous
Seasons for viewing:	Su, F
Map:	USGS Snoqualmie Pass 7.5′,
	USGS Chikamin Peak 7.5′,
	USGS Big Snow Mtn. 7.5′, and
	Green Trails #175, Skykomish

Getting There

Follow the driving directions under The Falls of Burnboot Creek and Getting to Goldmyer Hot Springs, on pages 167-168.

Trail and Falls

After checking in with the Goldmyer Hot Springs caretaker at the cabin, take the trail heading south through a clearing. (The caretaker can assist you.) After about a hundred feet, turn left (east) on a side trail and pass chunks of rusted machinery. In 0.2 mile the path leads to a campsite with a good view of the waterfall. The campsite itself was closed at the time of our visit because of a dangerously leaning tree overhead. Waterfall viewing from the site is permitted.

Burnboot Falls

Type of falls:	Slide/Plunge
Height of falls:	110 to 120 feet
Approach:	Hike 7.0 miles
Starting elevation:	2800 feet
Falls elevation:	2160 feet
Difficulty:	Strenuous
Seasons for viewing:	Su, F
Map:	USGS Snoqualmie Pass 7.5',
	USGS Chikamin Peak 7.5',
	USGS Big Snow Mountain 7.5',
	and Green Trails #175, Skykomish

Getting There

Follow the driving and trail directions under The Falls of Burnboot Creek and Getting to Goldmyer Hot Springs, on pages 167-168.

Trail and Falls

Check in with the Hot Springs caretaker. Follow the hot springs trail from the cabin to its end in 0.4 mile. Waterfall and bathing pools are nearly side by side. The best tree-strained views of the drop are from a stairway in the trail, at that point leading *down* to the Hot Springs.

   Expect nudity at the site. It is practically a given.

Pileated Woodpecker holes

Cougar Mountain

There are three waterfalls in the Coal Creek drainage, all within King County's Cougar Mountain Regional Wildland Park. (Coal Creek drains into Lake Washington.) The park is located in Newcastle, a residential community midway between Bellevue and Renton. It is just east of I-405 and is an equal distance south of I-90. Approaches from either interstate are possible.

From I-405, take exit 10. Follow largely green-belted Coal Creek Parkway for 2.4 miles to a left turn onto SE 72nd Street. In another 0.1 mile go left for 1.9 more miles on Newcastle-Coal Creek Road to the trailhead, signed Cougar Mountain Regional Wildland Park. This entrance is the park's Red Town trailhead, the western access to many miles of trails.

If approaching on I-90, take exit 13 and drive west on Newport Way to a left turn (south) at 164th Avenue SE. Drive the nearly two mile hill to a right turn onto Lakemont Boulevard. Follow it another 1.4 miles to the trailhead as described above.

There is a great deal more to do here than just viewing three waterfalls. Even if that is your only purpose, it is highly recommended that you obtain a park trail map. (The numerous trails are well-signed, but in their profusion they can be intimidating.) The map is available from King County Parks and also from many outdoor stores in the area.

Two of the three waterfalls included below, Far Country Falls and Coal Creek Falls, are satisfyingly reached via a loop of 5.4 miles, and the third by a round trip of only 0.6 mile out of the same trailhead's parking area.

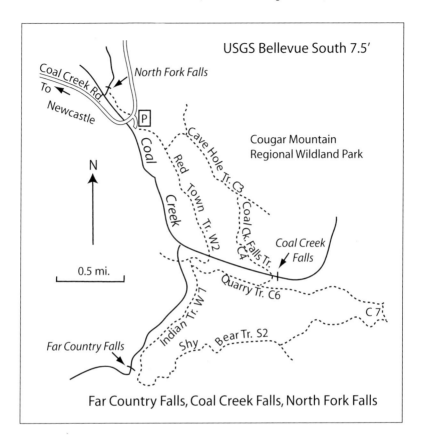

USGS Bellevue South 7.5'

Coal Creek Rd.

To Newcastle

North Fork Falls

P

Coal

Creek

N

Cave Hole Tr. C3

Red Town Tr. W2

Coal Ck. Falls Tr. C4

Cougar Mountain
Regional Wildland Park

Coal Creek
Falls

0.5 mi.

Quarry Tr. C6

C 7

Indian Tr. LM1

Shy Bear Tr. S2

Far Country Falls

Far Country Falls, Coal Creek Falls, North Fork Falls

Far Country Falls

Type of falls:	Flume/Tumble
Height of falls:	40 feet
Approach:	Hike 2.8 miles
Starting elevation:	600 feet
Falls elevation:	510 feet
Difficulty:	Easy
Seasons for viewing:	Sp, F, W
Map:	USGS Bellevue South 7.5'

Getting There

Follow the driving directions under Cougar Mountain.

Trail and Falls

From parking, walk left and uphill on Red Town Trail (W2). In 0.7 mile the way crosses Coal Creek and becomes the Indian Trail (W7). Follow the Indian Trail to the falls in 1.4 total miles. You will hear the falling water about a tenth of a mile after noting De Leo Wall Trail going off to the right. There is no sign at the short access trail to the moss-draped falls, but the right turn is easily spotted.

Coal Creek Falls

Type of falls:	Slide/Tumble
Height of falls:	40 feet
Approach:	Hike 2.8 miles or 5.4 miles
Starting elevation:	600 feet
Falls elevation:	875 feet
Difficulty:	Moderate
Seasons for viewing:	Sp, F, W
Map:	USGS Bellevue South 7.5'

Getting There

Follow the driving directions under Cougar Mountain, page 172.

Trail and Falls

Follow the trail directions to Far Country Falls. From there, continue south for only two-tenths of a mile on the Indian Trail to its junction with Far Country Trail (S1). Go left (east) on Far Country Trail. Shortly uphill the trail splits. Both forks go to Far Country Trail's junction with Shy Bear Trail (S2) in either two- or three-tenths of a mile, but the left fork, the longer one, first goes to Far Country Lookout. There are views out over the May Creek Valley and portions of the city of Renton, Lake Washington, and the southern end of the Olympic Mountains. Why not go left?

Continue on from the overlook and go left onto Shy Bear Trail (S2). The total mileage to the junction is 1.9 miles.

At 2.6 total miles, still on Shy Bear Trail (S2), note the Deceiver Trail coming in from the right. (One and fourth-tenths round trip miles out along

Deceiver Trail is another waterfall named Doughty. Due to its diminutive flow it was not rated. In high runoff, though, it might be a different story.) Continue along Shy Bear Trail to its junction with Fred's Railroad Trail (C7) at 3.4 total miles from parking. Go left (north) on Fred's, only to turn left again (west) on the Quarry Trail (C6) in one-tenth of a mile.

The Quarry Trail glides down to a right turn at 4.1 total miles onto Coal Creek Trail (C4). The way crosses its namesake creek in a short tenth of a mile just below the pretty falls.

On leaving the waterfall, continue northwesterly along Coal Creek Trail to its junction with Cave Hole Trail (C3). A left turn (still northwesterly) onto Cave Hole Trail brings you down to the Red Town Trail in half a mile. (Ignore "Red Town Creek Trail" along the way. It is not the way to parking.) Turn right on the Red Town Trail. Parking, and the 5.4-mile end of the loop, is two-tenths of a mile to the west.

North Fork Falls

Type of falls:	Veil
Height of falls:	23 feet
Approach:	Hike 0.6 mile
Starting elevation:	600 feet
Falls elevation:	540 feet
Difficulty:	Easy
Seasons for viewing:	Sp, F, W
Map:	USGS Bellevue South 7.5'

Getting There

Follow the driving directions under Cougar Mountain, page 172.

Trail and Falls

Walk west across the access road from parking for Cougar Mountain's Red Town trailhead. Coal Creek Trail runs along the northeast bank of the creek. Three bridges cross the stream in the short distance to the falls, all of which offer variations in getting to and from the attraction. Opposite the access for the first bridge is a small and intriguing cave entrance filled with clear, clean-looking water. Include the southwest bank approach on your way either to or from the falls, because on it there is a very informative signboard with text and photos explaining the coal-mining history of Newcastle. If you have noticed the slightly 'used' appearance of the land in the park, the photos alone will build appreciation for just how much the land has been able to recover from such intensive industrialization, i.e., abuse.

The third bridge moves the trail to the southwest bank. Shortly beyond it, a wood-railed fence provides a view site for the waterfall as it drops from a tributary directly into Coal Creek.

Olympic Peninsula

12,000 years ago ice sheets five thousand feet thick pushed down from the north and gouged out the inland arm of the sea we now call Puget Sound. From our present environmental perspective the resulting separation of landmasses has been a good one, for it has tended to keep the peninsula a good deal lighter in population than that of the Interstate-5 corridor.

US Highway 101 will be our guiding thread for this section. It crosses the five-mile-wide Columbia River at Astoria, Oregon before proceeding horseshoe-like around the Olympic Peninsula. It heads north along the coast of Washington and then east at Port Angeles, before swinging back south along Hood Canal to end near Olympia.

All waterfalls accessed from US 101 are presented starting in Aberdeen and proceeding north with ascending milepost numbers.

La Push Area

La Push is the center of fishing and residential activity of the Quileute Indian Nation. Though the public is welcome, First Beach is located on reservation land and is therefore subject to tribal authority. Other beaches and trails in the area are administered and maintained by personnel of Olympic National Park.

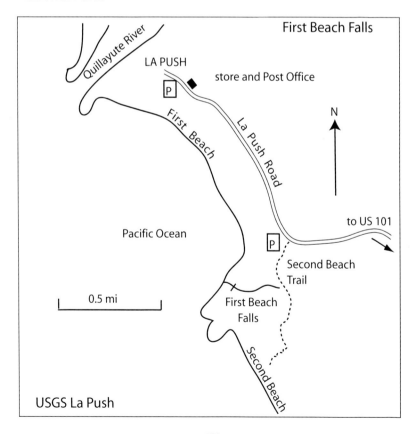

First Beach Falls

Type of falls:	Slide/Plunge
Height of falls:	100 to 110 feet
Approach:	Hike 2.0 miles
Starting elevation:	10 feet
Falls elevation:	120 feet
Difficulty:	Easy
Seasons for viewing:	Sp, F, W
Map:	USGS La Push 7.5'

Getting There

Five miles north of Forks, WA, turn west on SR 110, the La Push Road. Bear left at each of two Ys along the way, driving approximately 13.5 miles to La Push. Across from the community grocery store find a public parking area for First Beach.

Trail and Falls

First Beach is comprised of sandy oceanfront from the mouth of the Quileute River (not far west of the store) all the way southeast to where coastal cliffs begin. The waterfall streams from the first of these high rock faces. Seen from the end of sand-based viewpoints the falls are still somewhat distant, but forays over the tidal rocks for closer looks can be hazardous. If attempted, make certain that the tide is still receding.

Strawberry Bay Falls

Type of falls:	Plunge/Slide
Height of falls:	70 to 90 feet
Approach:	Hike 3.5 miles
Starting elevation:	230 feet
Falls elevation:	100 feet
Difficulty:	Strenuous
Seasons for viewing:	Sp, F, W
Map:	USGS Quillayute Prairie 7.5'

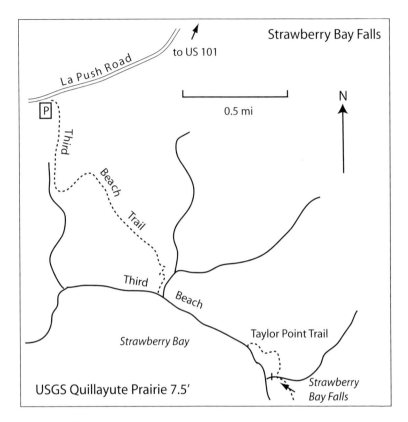

Getting There

Follow the driving directions for First Beach Falls (above). Drive 12.0 miles on SR 110 and park at the well signed Third Beach Trailhead on the left (south) side of the road.

Trail and Falls

Please note that the spellings *Quileute* and *Quillayute* both exist. USGS uses the latter on its 7.5' topo, Quillayute Prairie.

The well-maintained National Park trail drops only slightly then rises once more over the first mile. A final series of steep steps and switchbacks leads down to the remote beach. The waterfall is approximately four-tenths of a mile to the left (east) once on the sand. As with First Beach Falls, do not venture over the rocks to the base of the falls unless you are certain the tide is going out. Progress on the rocks is slow. Incoming tides have trapped more than one overly daring waterfall seeker.

Sappho

Beaver Falls

Beaver Falls

Type of falls:	Plunge
Height of falls:	15 to 20 feet
Approach:	Drive
Falls elevation:	580 feet
Seasons for viewing:	Sp, F, W
Map:	USGS Lake Pleasant 7.5'

Getting There

Leave US 101 very close to MP 204 in the barely perceptible town of Sappho, and go northeast on SR 113. Park on the right side of the road just after crossing Beaver Creek at 1.9 miles.

The Falls

This broad-fronted waterfall is visible from the road, but a short trail inside the guardrail leads to better views. At low flow rates, the drop is a study of segmented ribbons winding unhurriedly down the wide escarpment. When really rolling, it is a fascinating mini-Niagara seventy-five to one hundred feet in breadth.

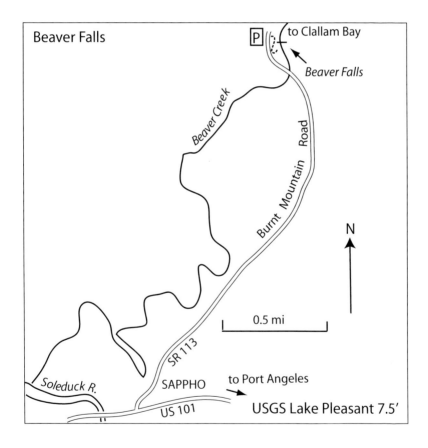

Beaver Falls

Hoko-Sekui

Without knowing it is happening it is easy to pass through Sekui. The same is true of Hoko while on the way to Lake Ozette. The lake, also within Olympic National Park, has some great boardwalk hikes out to ocean beaches.

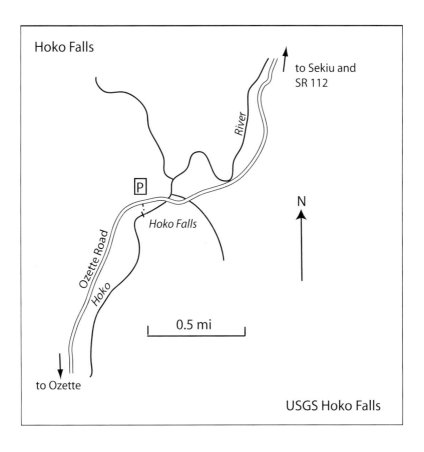

Hoko Falls

Type of falls:	Flume/Tumble
Height of falls:	10 to 12 feet
Approach:	Walk 0.2 mile
Starting elevation:	280 feet
Falls elevation:	215 feet
Difficulty:	Moderate
Seasons for viewing:	Sp, Su, F, W
Map:	USGS Hoko Falls 7.5'

Getting There

If coming up US 101 from Forks, or even from as far east of Forks as Lake Crescent, leave US 101 at Sappho, MP 204, and turn (north) onto SR 113. Pass Beaver Falls at the 1.9-mile mark and continue north. SR 113 ends into SR 112 at 10.0 miles. Approaching from Port Angeles on US 101, turn right (west) onto the eastern beginning of SR 112. The turn is about five and a half miles west of the city. SR 112 is signed for Clallam Bay and Neah Bay. Approximately thirty-five miles west of US 101, SR 112 intersects SR 113 coming up from Sappho.

From either the south or the east approach, restart your mileage count at the junction of State Routes 112 and 113. Continue generally west on SR 112 to Clallam Bay at 6.0 miles. Go west past Sekiu at 8.0 miles, and look for a prominent left turn (south) onto the Ozette Road at 10.3 miles. The Hoko River soon appears on the right and is crossed when 17.1 miles from the junction of SR 112 with SR 113. Park on ample road shoulders two-tenths of a mile south of the bridge.

Trail and Falls

The ravine of the Hoko River is impressively deep. Two-tenths of a mile south of the bridge, locate an unsigned – but also unhidden – old road entrance on the left (east) side of Ozette Road. It soon narrows to a rough path which drops moderately to the upstream end of a rock-walled canyon. Flat ledges at the base of the drop are easily accessible and make safe view sites.

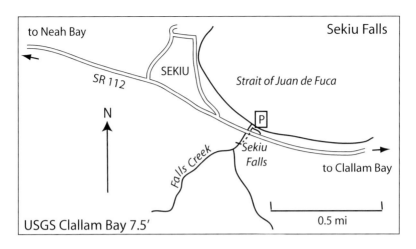

USGS Clallam Bay 7.5'

Sekiu Falls

Type of falls:	Slide
Height of falls:	20 feet
Approach:	Walk 0.2 mile
Starting elevation:	15 feet
Falls elevation:	60 feet
Difficulty:	Strenuous
Seasons for viewing:	Sp, Su, F, W
Map:	USGS Clallam Bay 7.5'

Getting There

Follow the driving directions for Hoko Falls. Approximately 1.8 miles west of the town of Clallam Bay turn right (north) into a large, unpaved parking area paralleling the Strait of Juan De Fuca. Follow this dirt strip back west to its end and park near the bridge over Falls Creek.

The turn into parking is unsigned. If you pass it, continue across the bridge and go a tenth of a mile uphill. A right turn there (north) goes into Sekiu. Use it to make a U turn, and then backtrack 0.2 mile.

Trail and Falls

This waterfall is also known as Falls Creek Falls, but should we perpetu-ate yet another falls with that all too common name? Walk beneath the

SR 112 bridge and pick up a somewhat nebulous trail upstream along the east bank of the creek. Sections have been covered over with washed-out gravel, and young alders necessitate some degree of dodging, but the path is there. The waterfall is just upstream of an old railroad bridge looking stout enough to still be holding a railroad car or two.

Low summer water levels may make this drop a better alternative season adventure.

Sol Duc Hot Springs Area

The Sol Duc Road, along with both Salmon Cascades and Sol Duc Falls, lies within Olympic National Park. Walking routes lead into the high country from many points along the fourteen miles of paved driving to the Sol Duc Falls trailhead. The road itself passes through marvelously preserved old growth forests. Do at least stop to visit the Hot Springs and its visitor center, described below.

Salmon Cascades

Type of falls:	Tumble
Height of falls:	35 feet
Approach:	Walk 0.1 mile
Falls elevation:	1300 feet
Difficulty:	Easy
Seasons for viewing:	Sp, Su, F, W
Map:	USGS Mount Muller 7.5'

Getting There

Drive US 101 to MP 219.2 and turn south on the Sol Duc Hot Springs Road. The turn is approximately twenty-nine miles west of Port Angeles and the same distance north of the town of Forks. Signed parking for Salmon Cascades is found on the right 7.1 miles from the beginning of Sol Duc Road. At times of high visitor traffic a National Park entry fee may be required.

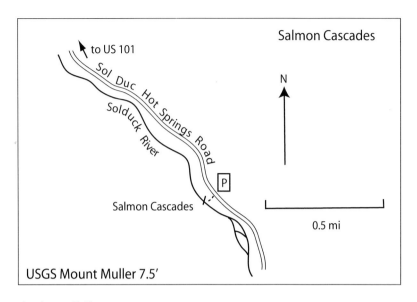

USGS Mount Muller 7.5'

Trail and Falls

A nicely kept path leads to an overlook of this embroiled, rocky chute in the Sol Duc River. The site once treated viewers to masses of salmon returning to birth waters in order to spawn. Sadly, few come any longer.

Sol Duc Falls

Type of falls:	Plunge
Height of falls:	30 to 40 feet
Approach:	Hike 2.0 miles
Starting elevation:	1900 feet
Falls elevation:	1960 feet
Difficulty:	Moderate
Seasons for viewing:	Sp, Su, F
Map:	USGS Bogachiel Peak 7.5'

Getting There

Approximately twenty-nine miles west of Port Angeles on US 101, or about the same distance north and east of the town of Forks, turn south on Sol Duc Hot Springs Road. The well-signed turn is at MP 219.2. Olympic National Park entrance fees may be required.

Sol Duc Falls

Drive 13.8 miles, much of it through virgin forests, to a huge parking area at the end of the road. Sol Duc Hot Springs resort and campground is passed at the twelve-mile point.

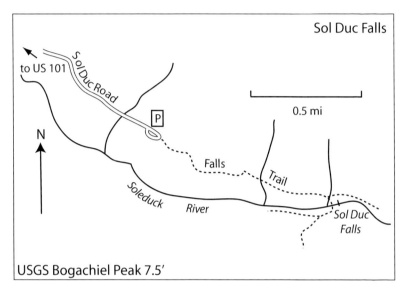

Sol Duc Falls

to US 101

Sol Duc Road

P

N

0.5 mi

Falls

Trail

Soleduck River

Sol Duc Falls

USGS Bogachiel Peak 7.5'

Trail and Falls

Despite the often distractingly large number of co-walkers to the picturesque falls, the passage through old growth bio-diversity on the way is stunning. (It is a conflicted feeling but the thought intrudes; in such a place one needs to be alone and silent.) The route is up and down, perhaps gaining and losing two hundred vertical feet each way. The trail forks just before it reaches the falls. The signed right branch drops to cross the Sol Duc River over its deeply incised run-out canyon. Views of the splendid triply-segmented drop are great from the footbridge, while different perspectives are offered at railed sites along the south bank of the river.

Lake Crescent

This clean, cold, and deep mountain lake lies on the northern fringe of Olympic National Park. Mountainous terrain squeezes its shores so tightly that for many years no road was built, and passage from one end to the other was by ferry. Fairholm, with its present day general store and restaurant, was the site of the west landing.

La Follette Falls

Type of falls:	Plunge/Slide
Height of falls:	200 feet
Approach:	Hike 1.8 miles
Starting elevation:	914 feet
Falls elevation:	1750 feet
Difficulty:	Strenuous
Seasons for viewing:	Sp, W
Map:	USGS Mount Muller 7.5', or Green Trails Lake Crescent #101

Getting There

Drive US 101 to MP 219.9 and park at an unsigned, cable-gated old mine road on the north side of the highway. To lend visibility, the padlocked cable is threaded through a length of white plastic pipe. The small gravel turnout is 0.7 mile east and downhill of prominently signed Sol Duc Hot Springs Road. It is also not far west of the Fairholm General Store at the extreme west end of Lake Crescent.

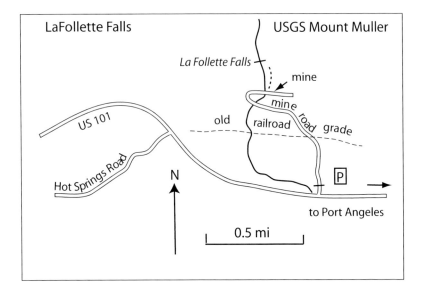

LaFollette Falls · USGS Mount Muller · La Follette Falls · mine · US 101 · old railroad · mine road grade · Hot Springs Road · N · P · to Port Angeles · 0.5 mi

Trail and Falls

The way begins as pleasant, drivable forest road. Halfway to the goal, however, it begins to degrade, for the route is that of a long abandoned mining road. At 0.2 mile the road diagonally crosses an equally aban-doned railroad bed, the right turn of which shows a fair amount of ve-hicle traffic. Go left (west) but soon angle to the right (northwest) away from the railroad grade and back onto the original mine road. At times the route becomes a foot trail that is variously stomped into landslides, routed over mine-tailings, and forced through washouts. A little search-ing may be necessary in one grassy clearing. With all of those problems, the track is still easy enough to follow.

At a bit under 0.5 mile, a sometimes-rampaging creek has wiped out the mine road and presented choices. (The creek is the unnamed host of La Follette Falls.) For choice one, go right and climb a hundred-fifty verti-cal feet of steep slip-and-slide mine tailings to rejoin the mine road. From there, a left turn (west) leads back to the same creek bed at an upper lev-el. (The lower of two mine openings is at the top of the tailings scramble.) For choice number two, cross the rocky breach in the old road and follow it up to the same higher creek crossing.

The latter route is rough and overgrown, but negotiable. On the up-per leg of the single switchback encountered you will find a horrendous jumble of blown-down trees that is best avoided. The blockage is visible from the approach to the turn, and boot tracks show how to avoid the biomess with a rarely excusable switchback cutoff.

Once at the upper creek crossing the choices are all steep, slippery, and backsliding, though not overly dangerous. From the mine road go up either bank of the creek, or, water level permitting, climb the creek bed itself. The reward is less than two-tenths of a mile upward.

La Follette Falls is a wet-season-only proposition, for its drainage is stingy with its moisture. Depending on snow levels, winter visits may be workable.

Marymere Falls

Type of falls:	Plunge
Height of falls:	90 to 100 feet
Approach:	Hike 1.6 miles
Starting elevation:	600 feet
Falls elevation:	980 feet
Difficulty:	Strenuous
Seasons for viewing:	Sp, Su, F, W
Map:	USGS Lake Crescent 7.5′

Getting There

From US 101 along the twisting east shore of Lake Crescent, about twenty miles west of Port Angeles and forty miles north and east of Forks, turn west toward the Storm King Ranger Station. At a T intersection, turn right to a loop parking area. There are public rest rooms at the site.

Trail and Falls

To the right of the rest rooms, take the paved walkway to and beyond the ranger station. At 0.2 mile the trail goes beneath US 101 via a large conduit. It then intersects a trail coming in on the right from Lake Crescent Lodge. Pass the Storm King Trail (left, at 0.4 mile) and reach another trail intersection at 0.6 mile. Go right and soon cross Barnes Creek on a flattened foot log equipped with a sturdy handrail.

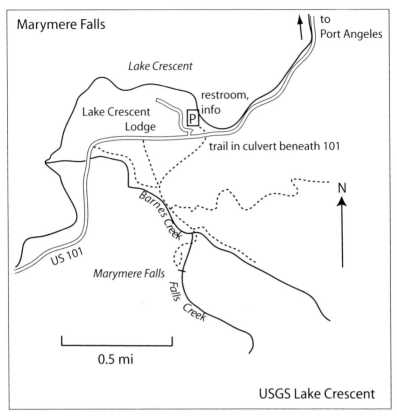

The trail now runs down the opposite bank of Barnes Creek to span close-by Falls Creek on a second well-engineered log. It then begins to climb steeply. The next trail split is both the beginning and end of a loop to two viewing levels of the pretty punch-bowl waterfall. Left is shorter and less demanding. Go either way, but at least return by the upper leg. There's room for disagreement here, but the upper viewing platform has a slight edge in scenic mood enhancement.

Olympic Hot Springs

The Olympic Hot Springs Road, at MP 239.6 of US 101 (nine miles west of Port Angeles) provides one of two major northern entrances to the wonders of Olympic National Park. The way follows the Elwha River south for half of its road miles before turning west to climb high on the valley shoulders of Boulder Creek. At road's end is the Appleton Pass Trail to Olympic Hot Springs as well as to a pair of pretty waterfalls.

Elwha River

Madison Creek Falls

Type of falls:	Slide/Plunge
Height of falls:	70 feet
Approach:	Walk 0.2 mile
Starting elevation:	260 feet
Falls elevation:	390 feet
Difficulty:	Easy
Seasons for viewing:	Sp, Su, F, W
Map:	USGS Elwha 7.5'

Getting There

Approximately nine miles west of Port Angeles on US 101 (or fifty-one miles north and east of Forks) turn south at MP 239.6 onto Olympic Hot

Springs Road. Stop at the Olympic National Park booth at 2.0 miles to pay the required entrance fee, then immediately turn left to park on the east side of the road for Madison Falls.

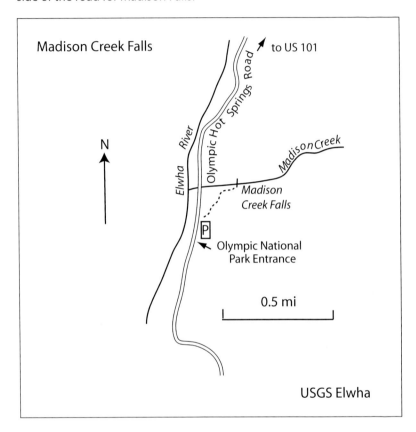

Madison Creek Falls

to US 101

Olympic Hot Springs Road

Elwha River

Madison Creek

N

Madison Creek Falls

P

Olympic National Park Entrance

0.5 mi

USGS Elwha

Trail and Falls

The walkway is paved all the way and is designed for wheelchair-bound persons. It is slightly uphill. There is a great deal of settlement history in the Elwha River valley, and park displays depict it nicely.

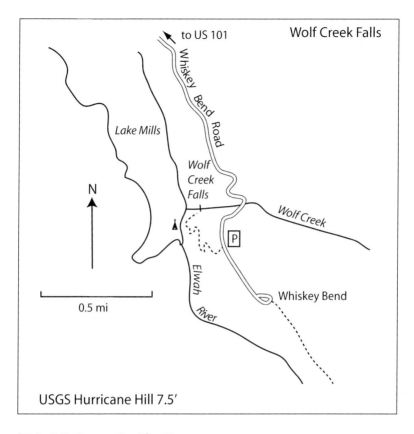

USGS Hurricane Hill 7.5′

Wolf Creek Falls

Type of falls:	Plunge/Slide
Height of falls:	30 feet
Approach:	Hike 0.9 mile
Starting elevation:	1100 feet
Falls elevation:	700 feet
Difficulty:	Strenuous
Seasons for viewing:	Sp, Su, F
Map:	USGS Hurricane Hill 7.5′

Getting There

Follow the driving directions for Madison Creek Falls. Two miles farther south on Olympic Hot Springs Road, a total of 4.0 miles from US 101 (and just beyond the Olympic National Park Elwha Ranger Station) turn left on gravel-surfaced, single-lane Whisky Bend Road. The road is steep and winding with sharp turns, so be sure to stay as far right as possible. At 8.0 miles total from US 101 park on narrow turnouts at the signed Lake Mills trailhead.

Trail and Falls

The trail switchbacks 0.4 mile down to where the Elwha River enters the impoundment of Lake Mills. Follow the river to the right (north) two hundred feet or so to the bank of Wolf Creek. The picturesque waterfall is visible just upstream in a darkened, foliage screened grotto.

Lower Boulder Creek Falls

Type of falls:	Plunge/Tumble
Height of falls:	30 to 60 feet
Approach:	Hike 6.9 miles
Starting elevation:	1820 feet
Falls elevation:	2600 feet
Difficulty:	Strenuous
Seasons for viewing:	Su, F
Map:	USGS Mount Carrie 7.5'

Getting There

Follow driving directions for Madison Creek Falls. Continue south on Olympic Hot Springs Road. At 4.0 miles from US 101, pass the Olympic National Park Elwha Ranger Station and drive on to Lake Mills at 5.6 miles. Olympic Hot Springs Road makes a tight curve to the right at Lake Mills dam, passing between a house and a barn on its way to parking at the end of drivable road 10.2 miles from US 101.

Trail and Falls

The Appleton Pass Trailhead is a major entry point for the interior of the Olympic Mountains. Expect competition for spaces in the seemingly ample parking area, and be ready for lots of company on the trail, at least as far as Olympic Hot Springs. Much of the first two miles of "trail" is on excellent-to-crumbling blacktop pavement, but stream wipeouts and sliding hillsides soon show why the trailhead has been reeled back to its present location.

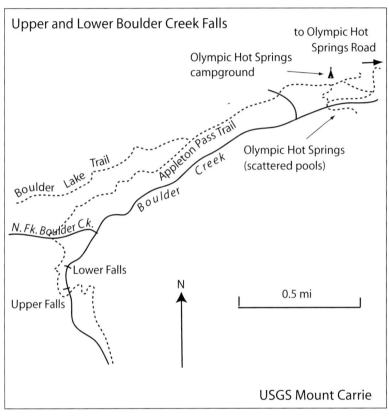

At 2.1 miles, where the road climbs right at a Y, another old road goes straight ahead to Olympic Hot Springs. It is two-tenths of a mile to the springs from the Y, but, because getting to the falls of Boulder Creek requires a good bit of energy, it is seems wise to consider visiting the hot dunking pools on the way back. There is a linking trail segment from the high ground above the Y.

Go up the right branch of the Y to another junction at 2.2 miles. Olympic Hot Springs Campground sites are found both to the right and left, but the Appleton Pass Trail goes left. Among the last of the campsites, and on the left side of the trail, look for the mentioned alternative "Hot Springs" trail sign. A little more than a half-mile west of the campground is yet another trail junction. Go left for the Appleton Pass Trail along the South Fork of Boulder Creek and to both Lower and Upper Boulder Creek waterfalls.

At 3.3 miles from parking the trail crosses the North Fork of Boulder Creek via a foot log. The log has no handrail, but is nicely flattened and has a girth large enough to lend good balance. When a tenth of a mile beyond the crossing, look for a signed side trail left and downhill. The creek and falls are found less than a tenth of a mile off the Appleton Pass Trail.

If the muses should be lurking anywhere within you, Lower Boulder Creek Falls could easily draw them out. The waterfall, as well as the stream itself, is a joy to behold.

If you intend to detour to the thermal pools, be on the lookout for the "Hot Springs" trail sign when back down to the Olympic Hot Springs Campground. The small sign is found toward the rear of one of the first tent sites found on the right. The spur drops steeply to an old road. Cross the road to a sturdy footbridge across Boulder Creek, and the path soon connects to numerous thermal seeps and dug-out shallow soaking pools.

Returning from the springs, turn right (east) after re-crossing the bridge. In two-tenths of a mile the old road leads back to the Appleton Pass Trail and on to parking in 2.1 miles. The detour to the springs adds only about three-tenths of a mile to the day.

The decision of whether to bathe or not needs to be based in part on the fact that there are no pre-bathing or toilet facilities at the springs, and that resultant bacterial counts in the pools are high. With regard to bringing children to the site, consider also that there is certain to be nudity along with non-sanctioned drugs and alcohol, all possibly in a party atmosphere.

Upper Boulder Creek Falls

Type of falls:	Plunge/Tumble
Height of falls:	100 feet
Approach:	Hike 7.3 miles
Starting elevation:	1820 feet
Falls elevation:	2800 feet
Difficulty:	Strenuous
Seasons for viewing:	Su, F
Map:	USGS Mount Carrie 7.5'

Getting There

Follow the driving directions for Lower Boulder Creek Falls. The trailhead is the same.

Trail and Falls

Upper Boulder Creek Falls is found just 0.2 mile (south) beyond the spur trail to Lower Falls. The upper descent is not signed, but is both heard and seen from the Appleton Pass Trail.

Viewing potential for Upper Falls is loaded with the often found and deadly combination of partial views with precipitous slopes. Please resist the attempt to get closer.

Quilcene to Shelton

Our waterfall tour of the Olympic Peninsula starts its home-stretch run close to where SR 20 begins and heads north to Port Townsend. US 101 turns south at that point, fulfilling its role as the only major highway on the east margin of the peninsula. From near Port Townsend, all the way to the city of Olympia, US 101 winds through the eastern foothills of the Olympic Mountains. The town of Quilcene is about thirteen miles south of US 101's junction with SR 20.

There are two land routes to Quilcene: For one, leave I-5 in Burlington, exit 230, and drive SR 20 to the Washington State Ferry from Keystone to Port Townsend. From the latter, follow SR 20 about 12.0 miles to a left (south) turn onto US 101. For the other, from Edmonds (to Kingston) or Seattle (to Bainbridge Island) take a Washington State Ferry across Puget Sound. Consult a Washington State road map and tie in to SR 104. It crosses Hood Canal by floating bridge and intersects US 101 at 9.0 north of Quilcene. Turn south onto US 101.

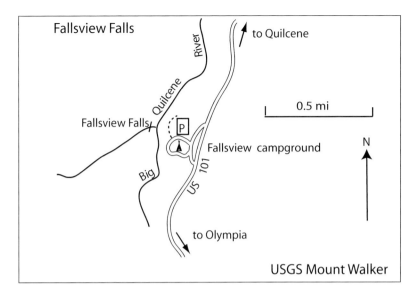

Fallsview Falls

Type of falls:	Slide
Height of falls:	110 to 160 feet
Approach:	Walk 0.1 mile
Starting elevation:	280 feet
Falls elevation:	250 feet
Difficulty:	Easy
Seasons for viewing:	Sp, F, W
Map:	USGS Mount Walker 7.5'

Getting There

Drive four miles south of Quilcene on US Highway 101. Turn right (west) into the Fallsview Campground at MP 298.3 and drive the loop to trail-head parking just west of campsite #24.

Trail and Falls

A short, level pathway leads to several viewpoints along a fenced over-look. Across the chasm, the waters of an unnamed creek plummet from unobservable heights to finish their journey in a long, graceful slide to the "Big Q", the Big Quilcene River.

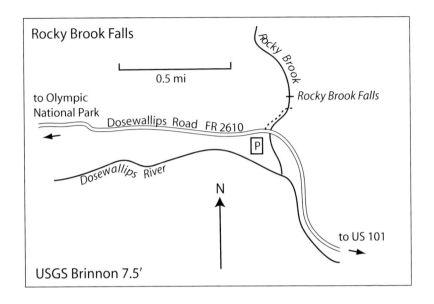

Rocky Brook Falls

0.5 mi

to Olympic National Park

Dosewallips Road FR 2610

Rocky Brook Falls

Dosewallips River

N

P

to US 101

USGS Brinnon 7.5'

Rocky Brook Falls

Type of falls:	Slide/ Tumble
Height of falls:	140 to 150 feet
Approach:	Walk 0.2 mile
Starting elevation:	440 feet
Falls elevation:	650 feet
Difficulty:	Easy
Seasons for viewing:	Sp, Su, F, W
Map:	USGS Brinnon 7.5'

Getting There

At MP 306 of US 101, just 0.4 mile north of the post office at Brinnon, turn west on the Dosewallips Road, signed for the Dosewallips Recreation Area. The road leads to sites in both Olympic National Forest and Olympic National Park. At 3.0 miles from US 101 the road crosses Rocky Brook. There is parking on both sides of Dosewallips Road at the west end of the bridge.

Trail and Falls

This is a popular place, and the wide, smooth 0.1 mile-long path reflects it. The potential width of the falls, judging by the band of exposed bare rock on both sides, is huge. Catch this one in high flow mode, for it can be commanding.

Constance Creek Falls

Type of falls:	Tumble/Plunge
Height of falls:	40 feet
Approach:	Drive, or hike 0.8 mile
Starting elevation:	1360
Falls elevation:	1510 feet
Difficulty:	Moderate
Seasons for viewing:	Sp, Su, F, W
Map:	USGS The Brothers 7.5'

Getting There

Follow the driving directions to Rocky Brook Falls. Where pavement ends on the Dosewallips Road the way becomes FR 2610. Reach a seasonal (see below) Olympic National Park gate at 12.7 miles from US 101. Constance Creek is crossed at 13.1 miles. Take care with parking along the road as there are no turnouts.

Between October and May the gate at the National Park boundary may be closed. If so, ample parking has been provided at the gate site. Waterfall-wise, the hike to two superb and very different cataracts is short and requires only a moderate investment of energy.

The Falls

Walking or driving, Constance Creek is only 0.4 mile inside the national park's seasonal gate. The waterfall is immediately on the right side of the road, north. This attraction will never be described using words such as highest, most powerful, thundering, or roaring. It is, however, a naturally artistic masterpiece. To most, the lovely tad of serendipity has been, before this recognition at least, only a bit of additional drive-by scenery on the way to other national park wonders.

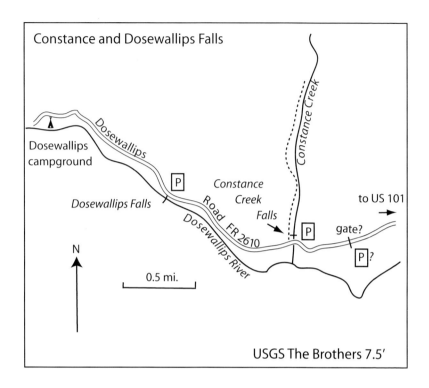

Constance and Dosewallips Falls

Dosewallips campground

Dosewallips

Dosewallips Falls

Road FR 2610

Dosewallips River

Constance Creek

Constance Creek Falls

to US 101

gate?

P

P

P?

N

0.5 mi.

USGS The Brothers 7.5'

Dosewallips Falls

Type of falls:	Tumble/Chute
Height of falls:	90 to 100 feet
Approach:	Drive, or hike 1.6 miles
Starting elevation:	1360
Falls elevation:	1420 feet
Difficulty:	Moderate
Seasons for viewing:	Sp, Su, F, W
Map:	USGS The Brothers 7.5'

Getting There

Follow the driving directions for Constance Creek Falls (above) and park in the large area outside the seasonal National Park gate. If the gate is open, drive on.

Dosewallips Falls

The Falls

Follow the walking directions for Constance Creek Falls as well. Walking or driving, Dosewallips Falls is only 0.4 mile west of Constance Creek on the Dosewallips Road, or 0.8 mile from the possibly closed Olympic National Park gate.

This waterfall merits all of the high-intensity words so out of place with Constance Creek Falls, for there is nothing delicate or artsy about Dosewallips. Here, a torrent of smokey-gray-green water pounds its many ways through a zigzagging maze of boulders and ledges.

Lake Cushman Falls

Type of falls:	Plunge/Tumble
Height of falls:	50 to 60 Feet
Approach:	Drive
Falls elevation:	840 feet
Seasons for viewing:	Sp, Su, F, W
Map:	USGS Hoodsport 7.5′

Getting There

Drive US 101 to MP 331.7 in the center of Hoodsport. Turn west on SR 119, also signed for Lake Cushman-Staircase. (Staircase is the name of the Olympic National Park Entrance at the end of the road.)

Look for a public viewpoint on the left at 6.2 miles. Have a great look up the lake to Timber Mountain and Lightning Peak, then drive on. Go left after a stop sign at 9.3 miles, still on SR 119 heading toward Staircase. After the pavement ends at 11.0 miles from US 101, watch for the waterfall on your right side (north). It appears very suddenly at the 11.7 mile mark. The gravel road is wide, so parking is plentiful on shoulders.

The Falls

Lake Cushman Falls is pressed tightly into a moss-lined and photogenic slot in a vertical wall, but the drop itself lacks something in scenic viability. A healthy, and therefore growing, tree is much in the way. Could be the waterfall was far nicer before the road builders chopped the wall.

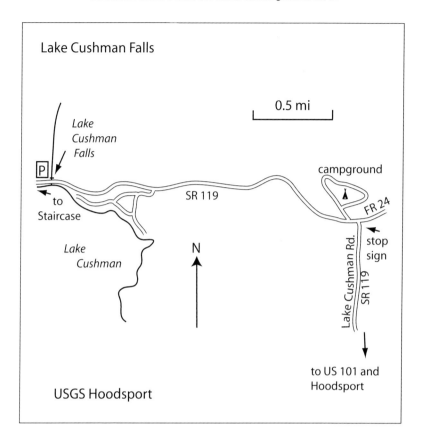

Kennedy Creek Falls

Type of falls:	Tumble/Plunge
Height of falls:	30 to 35 feet
Approach:	Hike 6.4 miles
Starting elevation:	8 feet
Falls elevation:	45 feet
Difficulty:	Moderate
Seasons for viewing:	Sp, F, W
Map:	USGS Kamilche Valley

Getting There
From I-5 take Olympia exit 104 and drive north on US 101. 4.5 miles north

of US 101's intersection with SR 8, turn left (west) onto a segment of Old Olympic Highway. At a total of 12.7 miles from I-5, park at the start of Road #2700, Kennedy Creek Road. The gated, gravel road is on the left (west).

Approaching from the north on US 101, turn right (west) at MP 356 and drive Old Olympic Highway less than a mile to Road #2700. Parking space is tight, so do not block the road entrance.

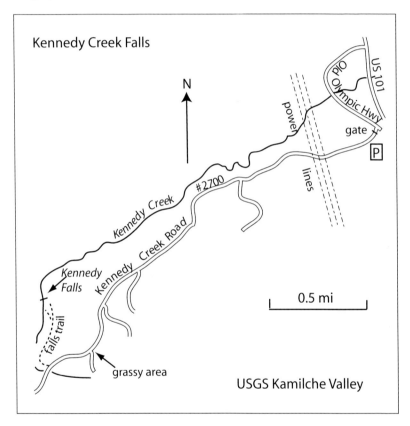

Trail and Falls

Road #2700 rises moderately for about 2.0 miles. It then stays close to 110 feet in elevation for another four-tenths of a mile. From there the road begins a sustained downhill run. Downward another tenth of a mile, 2.5 miles total, is, or was, a fork in the road system, but stay with the good gravel roadway. Two-tenths of a mile beyond, 2.7 miles total from Old

Olympic Highway, look for a well used path on the right (north) and turn into it. There is no sign. If the path is missed, Road #2700 soon crosses Kennedy Creek via a deeply buried culvert and starts uphill going west.

In less than a half mile of easy trail, though quite muddy at times, a sign indicates "Gravel Bar" to the left and "Falls" straight ahead. Go for the waterfall; it is found 3.2 miles from parking.

Kennedy Creek Falls is really two separate drops. The first, and most viewable, is a pretty little eight-foot tumble, one of those quiet spots that people like to think of as their secret place. The larger fall is just downstream at the entrance to a small, but respect-generating steep-walled canyon that is essentially un-viewable from its south bank. When water and energy levels permit, a creek wading and rough bushwhack along the north rim yields a look at the thirty-foot plunge. Do look to your safety; dense brush hides the lip of vertical drops thirty and forty feet to the creek bed below.

Marymere Falls, Lake Crescent, Olympic Peninsula

Resources

Highway Status Reports:

(800) 695-7623. Washington State Department of Transportation maintains this menu-driven, voice and dial-keypad-activated phone system. Be ready with the highway number you wish to know about. (I-5 is simply "5" and SR 530 is just "530".)

Maps:

Obtain USGS, Green Trails, and Custom Correct topographic maps at most outdoor stores.

The Custom Correct series, topographic hiking maps, covers the Olympic Mountains and beaches. Also try running stores, book stores, bicycle shops, and National Forest ranger and public service stations.

USGS:

Contact them for maps in three ways: (888) 275-8747, or email, ask@usgs.gov.

Order on-line using the USGS website, ask.usgs.gov. (Do not use the usual www. We didn't ask why.)

Maps may also be ordered on-line from:

Washington Trails Association, wta.org, click on "Our Store," bottom of the page. (Available only in sets of twelve from WTA online. Ten choices of sets.)

Metsker Maps:

They sell USGS and Green Trails maps plus countless other types.
Two locations:

7030 Tacoma Mall Blvd, Tacoma, WA 98409	253 474-6277
1511 1st Avenue, Seattle WA 98104	206 727-4430

R.E.I. Trip Planning:

Recreation Information Center, Trip Planning Section – R.E.I.,
222 Yale Avenue North, Seattle, WA 98109   206 470-4060

National Forests:

National Forest maps are indispensable for navigating the numerous and ever-changing pattern of logging and mining roads. Call the offices below to ask about maps and to get up-dated road and trail condition reports.

Ranger stations in the Mount Baker-Snoqualmie National Forest.
Note: "Public Service Centers" and "Visitor Centers" typically are open limited and/or seasonal hours. Call ahead to ask.

Darrington Ranger Station,
1405 Emmens Street, Darrington, WA 98241 — 360 436-1155

Glacier Public Service Center, (seasonal)
Glacier, WA 98244 — 360 599-2714

Mount Baker Ranger Station,
2105 State Route 20, Sedro-Woolley, WA 98284 — 360 856-5700
Trail Reports x515

North Bend Ranger Station,
42404 SE North Bend Way, North Bend, WA 98045 — 425 888-1421

Skykomish Ranger Station,
74920 N.E. Stevens Pass Highway, Skykomish, WA 98288 — 360 677-2414

Snoqualmie Pass Visitor Center, (seasonal)
PO Box 17, Snoqualmie Pass, WA 98068 — 425 434-6111

Verlot Public Service Center, (seasonal)
33515 Mountain Loop Highway, Granite Falls, WA 98241 — 360 691-7791

Olympic National Forest:

Hood Canal Ranger Station,
150 North Lake Cushman Road, Hoodsport, WA — 360 877-5254
Mail: Post Office Box 68, Hoodsport, WA 98584

Quilcene Ranger Station, Hood Canal District,
295,142 Highway 101 South, Quilcene, WA — 360 765-2200
Mail: Post Office Box 280, Quilcene, WA 98376

North Cascades National Park Website – Trail Information:

http://www.nps.gov/noca/planyourvisit/trail-conditions.htm   (206) 386-4495
ext. 11

Wilderness Information Center – Marblemount   (360) 873-4590 ext. 39

Mount Baker-Snoqualmie National Forest Website:

http://www.fs.fed.us/R6/mbs/recreation/activities/trails/

Tin Cup Joe Falls

Other Books by Robert L. Mooers

Waterfall Finder's Guide, Western Washington Series
Columbia River Gorge In Washington and Oregon
FallsGuy Trail Guides (Planned for 2008)

Waterfall Finder's Guide, Western Washington Series
The Southern Counties, including Mounts Rainier and St. Helens
FallsGuy Trail Guides (Planned for 2008)

Winter Hikes in Puget Sound & The Olympic Foothills
(1998)

Order Form

mail this form to:

FALLSGUY TRAIL GUIDES
715 12th Street
Bellingham, WA 98225

ITEM	PRICE	QUANTITY	SUBTOTAL
Waterfall Finder's Guide, #1	$16.95		
Winter Hikes in Puget Sound & The Olympic Foothills	$15.95		
		shipping & handling*	
		Sales Tax: 8.4%**	
		Total	

Please make all checks payable to: Robert L. Mooers

* U.S. shipping and handling rates: $4.00 for 1st book.

      Add $2 for each additional book to the same address.

** Sales Tax applies to orders shipped to Washington State.

Please visit our website:

www.fallsguytrailguides.com